Money Counts

**Studies in Social Analysis**
*General Editor: Martin Holbraad*
*University College London*

Focusing on analysis as a meeting ground of the empirical and the conceptual, this series provides a platform for exploring anthropological approaches to social analysis while seeking to open new avenues of communication between anthropology and the humanities, as well as other social sciences.

# MONEY COUNTS
Revisiting Economic Calculation

*Edited by*

Mario Schmidt and Sandy Ross

berghahn
NEW YORK • OXFORD
www.berghahnbooks.com

First published in 2020 by

**Berghahn Books**

www.berghahnbooks.com

© 2020 Berghahn Books

Originally published as a special issue of *Social Analysis,* volume 61, issue 4.

**Library of Congress Cataloging-in-Publication Data**

Library of Congress Control Number: 2019048212

**British Library Cataloguing in Publication Data**

A catalogue record for this book is available from the British Library.

ISBN 978-1-78920-684-5 (hardback)
ISBN 978-1-78920-685-2 (paperback)
ISBN 978-1-78920-686-9 (ebook)

# CONTENTS

# INTRODUCTION
## The Quality of Quantity: Monetary Amounts and Their Materialities

*Sandy Ross, Mario Schmidt, and Ville Koskinen*

Anthropologists rarely portray themselves as quantitative specialists or people who know about numbers. Instead, the adjective 'qualitative' plays a central role in our self-conception. We do qualitative fieldwork; we record and transcribe qualitative interviews; we are skeptical of quantifying methods—especially those of economists—which many anthropologists believe fall short of portraying rich lived worlds. In economic anthropology, this haste to distance ourselves from the disciplinary taboo—that-which-is-quantitative—has generated a division of labor wherein economists mathematically explore money's quantitative, abstract potential while anthropologists analyze money's qualitative aspects (Dupuy 2009; Peebles 2002). This situation neatly reproduces an economy-society binary that economic anthropologists and sociologists have struggled to overcome since the ostensible end of the formalist-substantivist debate (Hann and Hart 2011: 72–99). By avoiding quantitative methods and analyses, economic anthropology has largely abandoned the study of money's quantity and numbers.[1]

Different monies, despite having a diverse range of forms, shapes, and materials—coins, bank notes, stones, shells, and so on (Einzig 1951)—have often been

Notes for this section begin on page 13.

understood as conceptually similar, as sharing abstracting properties that spring 'naturally' from money's inherently quantitative nature (Bohannan 1959; Dalton 1965; Simmel [1907] 2011). If a form of money did not share this abstracting potential, it could be classified as special-purpose money, an object that seems money-like, but is not actual all-purpose money (Polanyi 1968). From this perspective, money's abstract potential must be tamed socially or culturally, in a realm that is positioned as outside of, or encompassing, economies (Parry and Bloch 1989; Graeber 1996; Karlstrøm 2014; Taussig 1980; Zelizer 1997).[2] The baby, money's quantity, has been thrown out with the bath water, money's abstracting potential.

However, the social sciences as a whole are in the midst of a quantitative turn. In contemporary economic anthropology, quantities—and to a lesser extent numbers—are associated with algorithmic trading and high finance; macro-economic phenomena, such as global crises and economic policies; and the ontology and epistemology of *homo oeconomicus*. Reinvigorated interest in quantitative approaches is largely focused on increasingly complex models and techniques for analyzing colossal data sets, but we believe that thinking about quantitativeness predominantly in terms of Big Data is a failure of imagination. We take inspiration from anthropologists (Almeida 1990; Ascher 2002; Boellstorff and Maurer 2015; Eglash 1997; Guyer et al. 2010; Mitchell 1980; Mosko and Damon 2005; Passes 2006; Peebles 2012; Saxe 2012; Urton and Llanos 1997), philosophers (Badiou 2008; Bateson 1979; Hacking 2014; Rotman 1993), science historians (Verran 2001), and sociologists (Day et al. 2014; Espeland and Sauder 2007; Gerlitz and Lury 2014) who have begun to explore the theoretical boundaries of this emerging quantitative turn. This edited volume argues that economic anthropology has a stake in the new quantitative frontier, not only through the study of high finance or quantitative methods with large data sets, but also through studies of diverse ethnographic and historical conceptualizations of money's qualitative quantities.

Chapters in this collection build upon recent emphasis on quantity as a central aspect of money (Akin and Robbins 1999; Guyer 2004; Holbraad 2005; Maurer 2008; Pickles 2013), rather than as a side effect of its use as a measure of value and medium of exchange. These contributions focus on exchanges that involve breaking down, calculating, dividing, and recombining sums of money—reconfiguring quantitative and physical heaps—to make new quantities that are qualitatively different. Rather than seeing money as a measuring stick, this book explores how money is used to make and symbolize quantities in different cultural contexts, and how such quantities can be qualitatively different and multiple. Peter Oakley's chapter presents historical and contemporary evidence of gold jewelry as a form of para-money, a substance whose material quantification—value by weight—could be easily assessed but artfully concealed in the form of the jewelry itself. The paradox of the money chain is its ambiguous status as a gift defined through its quantitative (weight) and material (purity) equivalences with money that might remain invisible for some actors. In other words, different monetary objects bring forth different practices that can prevent the achievement of or bring forth new forms of quantification.

Anna Echterhölter's chapter, for example, connects quantities and sensual experience: sounds, feats of strength, or seasonal changes. In her analysis of Frisian tax payments, as recounted by Jacob Grimm, she shows that these tax payments were assessed by the intensity and volume of sounds. Payments were adequate only if the collector, 12 rooms away, could hear coins sounding as they fell onto a shield. From Martin Fotta's chapter about contemporary Brazilian Gypsy men's monies, which become carefully quantified and ranked measures of masculinity, to Martin Holbraad's chapter about the two-tiered money economy in Cuba, which influences experiences of need and states of poverty, contributors to this volume are thinking ethnographically about how money's quantities are entangled with its qualities and physical forms.

Our introduction situates these insights in a broader theoretical context, explaining how contributors' analyses are related to some long-standing topics in mathematics: modes of divisibility; relationships between wholes and parts as understood through set partitioning; and hysteresis, which draws attention to non-linear, delayed qualitative transitions between quantitative amounts or states. We explore the concreteness of numerical quantities and offer novel ways to consider how quantities have, are, or index qualities. Our goal is not a comprehensive explanation of these phenomena. Rather, we hope to show how these chapters create and suggest illuminating analogies between mathematical ideas and ethnographic contingencies in the study of money, following Claude Lévi-Strauss's (1954: 585) suggestion that anthropologists should embrace "qualitative mathematics." Another main intellectual ancestor of ours is Marcel Mauss. In a famous, but often misunderstood, footnote in his *Essai sur le don*, Mauss ([1925] 2007: 94; our translation) wrote that money is an object that has "purchasing power, and this power is enumerated." Although much has been written on money's ability to buy things, on calculative devices in finance and business (Çalışkan 2007; MacKenzie and Millo 2003), and on calculation itself, whether 'rational' or otherwise, very little has been written on how the enumeration of money's purchasing power is negotiated by ordinary people in everyday life.[3] This book addresses that gap by exploring new dimensions of money's quantities.

## Modes of Divisibility: Arithmetic and Recursive Quantities

Jean Piaget's (1965) research on how children understand conservation of quantities can help explain differences between arithmetic and recursive divisibility. One of his experiments begins with two wide beakers containing equal amounts of liquid, let us say 200 milliliters. The contents of one beaker are divided equally between two tall, narrow glasses with 100 milliliters in each vessel. Children are then asked whether there is the same amount of liquid in the glasses as in the beaker. Those who recognize that the glasses and the beaker have the same quantity have understood the conservation of quantities. These children have perceived and accomplished an arithmetic division of quantity: one whole (the beaker's contents) is broken into two equal parts (the liquid in the two glasses). This is considered a mark of successful intellectual development. But there are also children who perceive the glasses as holding more liquid than the beaker. For those who follow Piaget, these children have failed to understand the conservation of quantities. However, these children have perceived a recursive division of quantity: one whole (the beaker's contents) has been transformed into two new wholes (one in each glass). These children perceive two wholes as more than one whole because two is more than one.

Arithmetic divisibility creates larger or smaller quantities of money through amalgamation (addition), expenditure (subtraction), and so on. Such money quantities are wholes composed of parts. In contrast, recursive divisibility creates whole quantities that are produced with and composed of other wholes, not parts. Borrowing from Helen Verran (2010: 173), we can understand recursively divisible objects as "having plurality contained within a unity." Recursively divisible sums are unique wholes composed of other equally unique wholes. We find an echo of this logic in Georg Simmel's ([1907] 2011: 195–196) *The Philosophy of Money*: "The unity of the sum of money that is paid for an object incorporates the values of all the elements of its uses, extending perhaps over a long period of time, as well as the particular values of its spatially separate parts and the values of all the powers and substances that prepared, and finally ended in, money." The materialization of money quantities, in this case as price, produces a whole that encompasses other potential wholes representing different expenditures or equivalences. Conversely, through arithmetical divisibility, money contains "unity within the plurality" (Verran 2010: 173). As a result of its numerical character, any amount of money stands in relation to all other amounts of money by being in a relationship with them through arithmetic functions such as addition, subtraction, multiplication, or exponentiation.

A focus on arithmetic divisibility is thus useful in ethnographic encounters where people are forced to translate different amounts from one currency or sphere of life to another. In his chapter, Emanuel Seitz rightly argues that how quantities of money are divided and recombined reflects highly specific forms of normatively and socially situated ethics and morals (Lazzer 2014; Ross 2014). To use money's quantity virtuously requires experience: it is a discipline requiring practice as well as a practice requiring discipline. In Sandy Ross's chapter, for instance, affluent migrants must learn how to use cash in ways that urban Russians find acceptable, such as making up payments with 'correct' combinations of denominations. Through trial and error, and sometimes with the assistance of local people, migrants come to understand how money quantities should be divided in particular settings and that not all money is always divisible. Money's quantity can also, as Echterhölter's chapter exemplifies, be mirrored in and shaped by the quantity of seasonal rhythms, growth, and decay. Fotta's contribution implies that the arithmetic approach to numbers must be divided further into a logarithmic and a linear understanding (Sun et al. 2012). Brazilian Gypsy men's loan repayment dates are based on logarithmic increases rather than linear ones: a 15-day term is followed by 30 days, but three months by one year. These logarithmic expansions reveal underlying logics of money's quantitative expansion.

Arithmetic dimensions of money's quantity play a further role in historic and ethnographic moments where money's numerical quantity takes on conceptual

(Seitz, this volume), economic (Braudel 1992; Weber [1923] 1981), or cosmological (Chu 2010) importance. The calculative potential of money's quantity can have repercussions in other social spheres (Apter 2014): a single token of money—a 1 shilling coin in Northwestern Tanzania (Weiss 1997) or a 5,000 ruble note in Russia—can symbolize the whole monetary economy. We suggest this is possible because of money's arithmetic divisibility. By engaging in real or speculative addition, subtraction, division, and multiplication, any part can be understood as being constitutive for diverse wholes, and any whole can be understood as composed of different parts.

While money's arithmetic potential and properties are widely discussed topics, money has rarely been considered as recursively divisible. This is surprising because monetary practices, even in finance and accounting, include many instances where wholes are composed of other wholes of the same status. Progressive taxation systems, for instance, divide one whole unit or sum—a citizen's total income—into brackets. Each bracket is a whole on which different rates of tax are paid. Let us consider the 2012–2013 tax contributions of an unmarried British citizen with a gross income of £60,000 who has no dependents and was born after 1948. This whole, £60,000, is composed of several other wholes. The first segment is an £8,105 personal allowance on which no tax is paid. The remaining amount, £51,895, falls within the basic rate and higher rate tax bands, which means it contains two further wholes: £34,370 taxed at 20 percent, and £17,525 at 40 percent. Each of these elements, for an accountant if not for a taxpayer, is a quantity whose importance is equal to that of the gross income. Thus, recursive understandings of quantity reflect some everyday realities in advanced capitalist economies. However, the unique ability of quantities to conceptualize the relations between parts and wholes is not only a mathematical matter. Money's quantities also become a medium for participation in other humans, the future, and divinities.

## Experiencing the Whole and Participating in Others

Holbraad's (2005: 247) concept of money as a "ground" that is able to "register displacement" is also concerned with relationships between parts and wholes. In his view, money's quantities are made visible and significant by reversing the assumed ground-figure configuration of monetary economies. Instead of goods being a whole from which money cuts a part, Holbraad suggests that amounts of money are wholes from which goods cut parts. Money is not only a transcendent means of calculation for comparing different objects; it is also a ground against which immanent expenditures appear as figures. In the moment of expenditure, any totality of money becomes a background that makes soon-to-be consumed sums meaningful. Thus, every amount of money is recursive, a whole containing other potentially qualitatively equal wholes. As each moment of expenditure reconfigures relationships between quantities, we can think of any monetary purchase as a form of self-reflexive bartering (ibid.: 244).[4]

Thus, despite money's multiplicity, expenditures cancel the possibility of other exchanges. This view is opposed to a conception of money as "unfettered empowerment" (Dodd 1994: 154) or as freedom (Simmel [1907] 2011: 214) that permits us to imagine many or even infinite potential expenditures. If we, however, follow Holbraad's analysis of money use in Cuban Ifá divination cults and understand quantities of money as part of figure-ground relations in which expenditure forecloses other options, then these figured quantities confront us with the potentially alien nature of our desires just as much as a divinity presents us with our unalterable fate. If a divinity informs us that we have no choice ("You really cannot choose between A and B. Your future depends on accepting A, and I suggest the sooner the better"), or if a commodity insinuates that we could not want or have anything else ("You imagine me as one of several possibilities, but in this moment, you only want me"), then quantities of money become revelatory objects. They inform us that we never truly wanted something else in the first place.

Thus, we agree with Noam Yuran's (2014: 8) suggestion to understand money as an "object of desire" that "underscores the extent to which our own desire is foreign to us." Yuran uses Dickens's industrialist from *Hard Times*, Josiah Bounderby, to consider how others' perceived desire for money shapes relations of power. When his employees demand better wages, Bounderby believes they are trying to 'steal' his money to live luxuriously. These desires that Bounderby projects onto the workers allow him to justify the cruelly exploitative working conditions in his factory. Fears about others' desire to appropriate his money shapes Bounderby's relationship with his wealth: "Bounderby imagines that his workers desire excessive pleasures that he himself conspicuously avoids" (ibid.: 85). Having identified luxury and desire as pathological, Bounderby excludes his employees from basic subsistence and himself from enjoying his money, which is exhaustively signified by the desires of his employees.

Placing desires unknown to ourselves or the unknown desires of others at the heart of money's conceptualization is a fascinating way to square the concept of money and notions of personhood in anthropology. Precisely because an amount of money allows its owner to imagine it both as a known whole with unknown parts and as a known part of an unknown whole, it enables us to participate in unknown dimensions of ourselves, goods, and other humans or geographical and ontological spheres without necessarily being acquainted with or already a part of them, and vice versa. This is impossible in context-bound gift exchanges where the impartibility of the given object symbolizes the impartibility of the represented and established social relation (Godelier 1999). An example is the famous *symbolon*, a material object serving as a pledge by being cut into two halves, with both parties of the agreement keep one-half (see Seitz, this volume). In contrast, money is a medium of participation in unknown others (Simmel [1907] 2011: 210), unforeseeable futures, and the untouchable divine. However, this is only possible through money's quantitative properties.

If money were neither partible nor multiple, we could neither trust in our own monetary wealth's hidden potentials nor identify a single coin as a sign of future affluence. Thus, money's quality of quantity allows it to function as the ground on which social relations of Brazilian Gypsies emerge (Fotta, this volume); enables Dholuo-speaking Kenyans to imagine and calculate with amounts they currently do not possess (Schmidt, this volume); helps families or individuals to compensate for death or injury (Echterhölter, this volume); and lets migrants pass 'impartial' judgment on, yet see themselves as participating in, urban Russian society (Ross, this volume). In the case of Cubans' struggles in a dual currency economy (Holbraad, this volume), the simultaneity of the dollar's absence and its presence reminds poor Cubans that they, although intricately entangled with it, are ultimately excluded from the consumerist benefits that 'others'—rich Cubans as well as Americans—enjoy. In an attempt to fulfill their desires nevertheless, poor Cubans internalize the external division between the dollar and the peso economy through window-shopping and in the experience of need.

## Set Theory and Boundless Recursivity

The infinity of monetary desire is an old topic in academic debates and artistic approaches to money. Both the continuously growing amounts of gold that Scrooge McDuck hoards in his money vault and Simmel's ([1907] 2011: 253) "endless series of possible volitions, self-developing actions and satisfactions" illustrate how infinity, often masked as abstraction, plays a central role in money's conceptualization. However, we rarely consider how finite amounts of money permit these experiences of infinity. Set partitioning, an element of mathematical set theory, helps us understand how a finite amount of money—an investment banker's £200,000 bonus—can seem like an infinite quantity. Furthermore, it illustrates how desire and recursivity are entangled through monetary quantities.

Set theory is a foundational branch of mathematics. Sets are groups of objects, known as elements. Sets are defined by common attributes of their elements. For example, $A_9$ is a set containing all positive integers between 1 and 9: $A_9 = \{1, 2, 3, 4, 5, 6, 7, 8, 9\}$. However, elements need not be numbers or quantities; they can be any arbitrary object or even other sets. A set consisting of fluffy objects could contain plush toys, clouds, and bouffant hairstyles. Set theory does not discriminate between qualities and quantities. Sets may also contain an infinite number of elements, such as all real numbers between 0 and 1. Set partitioning deals with how sets are divided into mutually exclusive subsets and/or single elements. $A_9$ can be partitioned many ways. We could divide it in two subsets, even and odd integers: $\{\{1, 3, 5, 7, 9\}, \{2, 4, 6, 8\}\}$. We could make two subsets, one containing multiples of 3, and another containing the remaining elements: $\{\{3, 6, 9\}, \{1, 2, 4, 5, 7, 8\}\}$. As the number of elements grows, the number of potential partitions increases rapidly. This increase is more than exponential. Bell numbers ($B_n$) express the number of potential partitions in a finite n-element set. The set $A_9$, for instance, can be partitioned in $B_9 = 21{,}147$ ways. Sets of infinite size can be partitioned in an even bigger infinite number of ways.

With respect to money, set partitioning provides a mathematical foundation for understanding how a finite quantity can seem like infinite possibility. We can think of $1,000 as an interval on the real number line, containing all real numbers between 0 and 1,000. Splitting the interval in two parts, or any number of parts, can be done at infinitely many points. Alternatively, we can think of $1,000 as a set of all amounts between $0.00 and $1,000.00, down to the level of a penny. In this case, there are 99,999 different points—at any penny—where the total can be divided in two parts. In financial markets, even fractions of the smallest denominations may be used, creating more division points. Thus, a quantity of money permits seemingly boundless partitioning.

We can apply these insights from set partitioning to further conceptualize Simmel's image of money ("endless series of possible volitions") as a set with three elements: an almost infinitely partible quantity of money, a huge variety of goods potentially bought with the whole sum or wholes within it, and moments of an infinitely partible time in which these goods are purchased. With this logic, we can then understand how even a small amount of money, perhaps $10, can be divided into an "endless series" of different purchases in future moments (Schmidt, this volume). In other words, as recursive quantitative wholes of potential expenditures, both little quantities like $10 and bigger quantities such as $100 or $1,000 can be spent in infinitely different ways.

Set partitioning, however, not only allows us to understand that $10 and $100 are quantitatively comparable because they both enable infinitely diverse ways of purchasing goods. It also helps us to understand why a larger sum does not necessarily encompass smaller amounts. While the quantity of $10 is arithmetically included in the quantity $100, when we conceive of an amount of money as a set of purchasing potentials, these two sums are both quantitatively similar and qualitatively different. Quantitatively, $10 and $100 are similar because both allow the experience of an infinite diversity of purchases. But qualitatively, these two quantities are different because the internal structures defined by the partitioning of $100 and $10 are not equivalent and cannot be grasped by arithmetic means. Put another way, giving away $10 of $100 'feels' quite different from giving away $10 from $1,000 or even $100 from $1,000. One sum is simply bigger, as one shade of green is greener than another. Monetary amounts thus bypass the difference between countable multitudes—assessed with numerical, arithmetic tools—and continuous magnitudes, whose extent can only be estimated. They are both numerical, like numbers, and material, like colors (Schmidt, this volume).

Set partitioning considers how finite quantities of money can seem infinite. But several contributors to this edited volume—notably Fotta and Oakley—are concerned with transitions in the other direction, from boundlessness to finitude or even worthlessness. Fotta, for example, examines how quantities of money are transformed into measures of masculine potency and influence. His chapter examines how, why, and when economic registers of value are transferred to political spheres of valuation. Among Brazilian Gypsy men, money quantities and materialities are entangled and transformed together, but in ways that complicate boundary drawing between different qualitative states because transitions are delayed and boundaries are elastic. We use the hysteresis effect—a concept used by physicists to capture lags between changed conditions and changed states—and the sorites paradox, also known as the paradox of the heap, to examine the importance of past qualities for understanding current quantities.[5] The hysteresis effect helps us to interpret the sorites paradox in a way that offers new insights into delayed transformations between qualitative states marked by elastic quantity thresholds.

## Delayed Transitions, Elastic Thresholds, and Hysteresis

In the sorites paradox, we begin with a heap of sand. If we take away a single grain, the quantity remains a 'heap'. In Holbraad's terms, the figure fails to stand out against the ground because the amount removed is too small. But if we continue to remove grains of sand, when does the remainder become a non-heap? When does the grain of sand become a visible figure against the ground of the pile? If we think of the heap in terms of recursive divisibility, it would consist of many fairly similar wholes combined into a larger entity. Thus, we are seeking the moment when a whole—the heap—can no longer sustain its integrity as a meaningful amalgamated quantity.

The sorites paradox therefore becomes a problem about material transformations between states. When is a quantity of high-purity gold worth more, or possibly less, than its weight? When do the inhabitants of the Western Kenyan market Kaleko perceive of a sum of money as finite instead of infinite? When does an additional Gypsy loan transform from a mere transfer of pecuniary wealth into a measure of influence and masculine power? The transition between being a man who loans some money and being a potent man who loans great sums of money is neither binary nor instantaneous. There is no threshold up to which men must loan in order to acquire or demonstrate strength (*força*). Rather, how much is owed to someone today is compared to how much was borrowed in the past, how much he owes to others, how much he has borrowed previously, how much he has gained in marriage, and how well he provides for his family. Slowly, a Gypsy man builds his *força*, but the moment he becomes a strong man arrives some time after he has built up the requisite money circulations. We suggest such temporal lags and delayed transformations between qualitative and quantitative states can be explained rather well with hysteresis.

Hysteresis is a concept used by physicists to describe how an object's or system's current state depends on a sequence of past conditions that lead up to it. A thermostat and heater are designed to exhibit hysteresis. When a thermostat is set at 18°C, whether or not it activates the heater depends on the previous temperature of the room as well as its current temperature. If the room were 17°C but had previously been 18°C, the heater will not activate until the temperature drops a bit more. But if the room was previously 16°C, then the heater would remain active until the temperature rises to 19°C. For the thermostat to activate or deactivate the heater, the room's recent temperature history is just as important as whether the most recent temperature shift was upward or downward. This temporal aspect, or memory of past events, influences how near or far the threshold is to the adjacent state. Hysteresis therefore allows us to focus on qualitative transformations that are triggered by a quantitative decrease or increase but do not occur immediately. This concept frames how past quantities shape current qualitative assessments.

But how do thermostats relate to the sorites paradox? We must redefine our knowledge of the heap's materiality and quantities. If we knew that there was previously a heap of 5,000 gold doubloons and took away one coin at a time so that there were only 4,000, the quantity would appear somewhat diminished. By the time there were only 1,000 coins left, the pile would seem significantly diminished. We would still have a heap, but we would be aware that our quantity of money was approaching a non-heap. There is a flexible boundary between the heap and the non-heap, or one material state and the next. But our awareness that the quantity used to be bigger would lead us to redefine the remainder as a little heap or maybe just a collection. But if we suddenly receive a windfall of 2,000 doubloons, we would have a heap once more. As the bundle dwindles, its quality of heapness somehow remains. Yet once it has become a non-heap, achieving the status of a heap once more takes a significant input. Alternatively, if we began with 500 doubloons, which we perceived as a heap, and accumulated more and more until we had 5,000, the resulting treasure hoard might seem like many coin heaps rolled into one. There is not a fixed boundary between heap and non-heap. Instead, there are elastic thresholds where heapness depends on whether there has recently been accumulation or depletion. Hysteresis thus highlights the importance of past perceptions and the nature of the quantitative change on qualitative evaluations and draws our attention to the immediate past and its long shadow in the present.

If money is memory, as Keith Hart (2000) has argued, then hysteresis provides a way of considering how qualitative estimations of current money quantities are shaped by memories of former quantities and the qualities attached to them. Time becomes visible as the ground against which material, qualitative, and quantitative changes and flexible thresholds are defined, as exemplified by François Simiand's (1932) observation that workers perceive an increase in the absolute numerical value of their salary as more money even if their purchasing power simultaneously decreases. Our interests as scholars of money is in finding moments where quantities and qualities are transformed with temporal lags. This is not about reflexive measures that constitute what they index; rather, it is about discerning turning points in physical and qualitative transformations that are entangled with quantities. This approach is not opposed to that of scholars studying ordinal rankings (Guyer 2004, 2010) or ranking algorithms and metrics (Espeland and Sauder 2007). We are concerned with transformations between qualitative or physical states, whereas work on the reflexivity of metrics and rankings is concerned with competition and variable gaps between ranks (Guyer 2010) and the calculations behind ratings (Gerlitz and Lury 2014). Guyer in particular has highlighted how distance between intervals increases (between some points, seemingly exponentially) at the upper end of a ranking scale. This insight helps us understand why it is harder to move from fifth to third position in such a scale than from seventy-fifth to seventieth. With rankings, thresholds between positions are defined by another person's algorithmic evaluation or performance. Although new records may be set, the new thresholds remain fixed hurdles that others must overcome. In contrast, we are interested in elastic changes and boundaries, like bidding increments in an auction, rather than fixed thresholds, like the rank ordering of the auction bidders and their bids. A hysteresis-informed approach is suited to thresholds that recede or come nearer depending on previous quantities and qualities, rather than the set hurdles of metrics and scales. This perspective is more relevant to monetary quantities that are entangled with qualities, where boundaries between states are more like shades of color that blend.

## Introduction to the Chapters

In this introduction, we have tried to show how the historic and ethnographic challenges examined in these chapters relate to blurred quantity-quality boundaries. Drawing on ideas from mathematics and physics that are inspired by our contributors' approaches, we have further attempted to provide several different entry points or frames through which their chapters can be read. We begin with Oakley's chapter, which asks whether gold jewelry can be money. In his response to this question, Oakley reminds us of the continuing importance of money's diverse substances, especially when those substances have other uses. In his examples of gold musters melted down as scrap and Tudor money chains, Oakley highlights how gold as a substance slips between registers of quantitative valuation—as jewelry, as a pile of tangled metal, and as para-money.

Echterhölter's chapter picks up on this theme of quantities that are expressed through substances and qualities. Drawing on Jacob Grimm's accounts of rural Germanic law and legal customs, she connects quantification and measurement, then presents a mode of quantification without numbers. Quantities can be expressed 'poetically' with images that define relationships between quantities through objects, living things, and cycles of growth. These quantifications present measures that are open to negotiation. Rather than being accurate—producing measures of a 'true' quantity—these measures, and the procedures that create them, are precise. They reliably produce similar results, even when elements of chance are introduced. Oakley's and Echterhölter's chapters thus offer two views of qualitative quantification, one based around substances and divisibility, the other built on poetic images or qualitative measurement procedures with elements of chance.

Ross's chapter also examines blurred boundaries between quantities and qualities. She explores how affluent migrants in Moscow and St. Petersburg struggle to domesticate the ruble's seemingly large quantities through qualitative means, turning quantities into evidence that justifies or legitimates fears or moral judgments about Russian culture and society. The symbolic potential of money's quantity and its ability to mediate the participation of actors with one another are equally central to Schmidt's contribution. Schmidt argues that money's recursivity—its capacity to be a whole composed of equally significant wholes—enables Dholuo-speaking Kenyans to experience freedom of actions. Yet money's mathematical divisibility, linked to required expenditures and fixed (often inadequate) resources, relates the concept of money, as well as individual tokens of it, to coercion and life's pitfalls.

Like Schmidt's contribution, the chapters by Fotta and Holbraad explore themes around marginality and money. For Holbraad, Cuba's two-tiered money economy of dollars and pesos creates different experiences of need and privation. He argues that quantitative commensuration becomes an inextricable part of qualitative moral struggles and discourses about inequalities. Fotta's chapter brings us full circle, sharing Holbraad's and Schmidt's focus on money and poverty. His account of informal moneylending among Calon men furthermore presents money's quantities as indexes of masculinity. On one hand, this links Calon men's conceptualization of money's quantity with Calon cosmology and morality; on the other, it exemplifies how money's quantity can relate to allegedly non-quantitative spheres of social life.

Before Nigel Dodd summarizes the contributions in his afterword against the background of the quantity-quality divide, Emanuel Seitz's chapter provides a provocative, wide-ranging dialogue on money's immaterial and quantitative nature. Seitz interrogates the shifting place of money's quantity in the history of economic thought, linking his discussion to diverse themes explored ethnographically in the other chapters. He demonstrates that these chapters should not be read as counter-hegemonic descriptions of how various 'others' conceptualize money's quantity, but rather as examples of the immense potential of a type of ethnography that does not flinch from philosophically rethinking its basic concepts. Thus, we do not shy away from our conclusion that recursive and other 'alien' understandings of quantity explored in this edited volume entail correct and true statements about quantity and its qualitative and material manifestations. As such, we hope to pave the way for further explorations of money's quantity and to offer a way out of theoretical and practical dead ends.

## Acknowledgments

The editors thank the German Research Foundation's research training group "Value and Equivalence" (1576/2) for generously supporting a workshop upon which this book is based. Sandy Ross thanks Celia Lury and Nigel Dodd for their encouragement to write on new approaches to money quantities and the quantitative turn. Mario Schmidt is grateful to Marin Trenk, who sparked his interest in the anthropology of money.

**Sandy Ross** has been a Senior Lecturer at Leeds Beckett University and a Sociology Fellow at the Higher School of Economics. She is currently exploring new options outside academia, particularly in policy research. With Chris Swader, she is editing a forthcoming issue on post-socialist moral economies for the *Journal of Consumer Culture*.

**Mario Schmidt** is a Postdoctoral Fellow at the a.r.t.e.s. Graduate School for the Humanities, University of Cologne. He currently explores the interdisciplinary potential between anthropology and behavioral economics. He has published in journals such as *Africa*, *Ethnohistory*, and *HAU: Journal of Ethnographic Theory*.

**Ville Koskinen** is an applied statistician and computer scientist currently employed in bioinformatics software development. His professional interests range from the design of algorithms and statistical modeling in proteomics to survey design and exploratory data analysis in sociology.

## Notes

1. Notable exceptions to this tendency include Crump (1978), Guyer (2004), Lave (1988), Mauss ([1925] 2007), Mimica (1988), Rosin (1973), and Strathern (1992).
2. See Maurer (2006) for an overview of the anthropology of money.
3. For exceptions, see Cochoy (2008) and Rosin (1973).
4. For more on this form of self-reflexivity, see the chapters by Holbraad, Ross, and Schmidt in this volume.
5. See Bourdieu ([1977] 1980) for a different application of hysteresis.

## References

Akin, David, and Joel Robbins, eds. 1999. *Money and Modernity: State and Local Currencies in Melanesia*. Pittsburgh, PA: University of Pittsburgh Press.

Almeida, Mauro. 1990. "Symmetry and Entropy: Mathematical Metaphors in the Work of Lévi-Strauss." *Current Anthropology* 31 (4): 367–385.

Apter, Emily. 2014. "Shareholder Existence: On the Turn to Numbers in Recent French Theory." *Textual Practice* 28 (7): 1323–1336.

Ascher, Marcia. 2002. *Mathematics Elsewhere: An Exploration of Ideas Across Cultures*. Princeton, NJ: Princeton University Press.

Badiou, Alain. 2008. *Number and Numbers*. Trans. Robin Mackay. Cambridge: Polity Press.

Bateson, Gregory. 1979. *Mind and Nature: A Necessary Unity*. New York: Hampton Press.

Boellstorff, Tom, and Bill Maurer, eds. 2015. *Data: Now Bigger and Better!* Chicago: Prickly Paradigm Press.

Bohannan, Paul. 1959. "The Impact of Money on an African Subsistence Economy." *Journal of Economic History* 19 (4): 491–503.

Bourdieu, Pierre. (1977) 1980. *Le sens pratique*. Paris: Editions de Minuit.

Braudel, Fernand. 1992. *Civilization and Capitalism, 15th–18th Century*. Vol. 2: *The Wheels of Commerce*. Trans. Siân Reynolds. Berkeley: University of California Press.

Çalışkan, Koray. 2007. "Price as a Market Device: Cotton Trading in Izmir Mercantile Exchange." *Sociological Review* 55 (2): 241–260.

Chu, Julie Y. 2010. "The Attraction of Numbers: Accounting for Ritual Expenditures in Fuzhou, China." *Anthropological Theory* 10 (1–2): 132–142.

Cochoy, Franck. 2008. "Calculation, Qualculation, Calqulation: Shopping Cart Arithmetic, Equipped Cognition and the Clustered Consumer." *Marketing Theory* 8 (1): 15–44.

Crump, Thomas. 1978. "Money and Number: The Trojan Horse of Language." *Man* (n.s.) 13 (4): 503–518.

Dalton, George. 1965. "Primitive Money." *American Anthropologist* 67 (1): 44–65.

Day, Sophie, Celia Lury, and Nina Wakeford. 2014. "Number Ecologies: Numbers and Numbering Practices." *Distinktion* 15 (2): 123–154.

Dodd, Nigel. 1994. *The Sociology of Money: Economics, Reason and Contemporary Society*. Cambridge: Polity Press.

Dupuy, Francis. 2009. "Les 'monnaies primitives': Nouvelles considérations." *L'Homme* 190 (2): 129–151.

Eglash, Ron. 1997. "When Math Worlds Collide: Intention and Invention in Ethnomathematics." *Science, Technology & Human Values* 22 (1): 79–97.

Einzig, Paul. 1951. *Primitive Money in Its Ethnological, Historical and Economic Aspects*. London: Eyre & Spottiswoode.

Espeland, Wendy N., and Michael Sauder. 2007. "Rankings and Reactivity: How Public Measures Recreate Social Worlds." *American Journal of Sociology* 113 (1): 1–40.

Gerlitz, Carolin, and Celia Lury. 2014. "Social Media and Self-Evaluating Assemblages: On Numbers, Orderings and Values." *Distinktion* 15 (2): 174–188.

Godelier, Maurice. 1999. *The Enigma of the Gift*. Trans. Nora Scott. Chicago: University of Chicago Press.

Graeber, David. 1996. "Beads and Money: Notes Toward a Theory of Wealth and Power." *American Ethnologist* 23 (1): 4–24.

Guyer, Jane I. 2004. *Marginal Gains: Monetary Transactions in Atlantic Africa*. Chicago: University of Chicago Press.

Guyer, Jane. 2010. "The Eruption of Tradition?" *Anthropological Theory* 10 (1–2): 123–131.

Guyer, Jane I., Naveeda Khan, Juan Obarrio et al. 2010. "Introduction: Number as Inventive Frontier." *Anthropological Theory* 10 (1–2): 36–61. Special section titled "Number as Inventive Frontier."

Hacking, Ian. 2014. *Why Is There Philosophy of Mathematics at All?* Cambridge: Cambridge University Press.

Hann, Chris, and Keith Hart. 2011. *Economic Anthropology: History, Ethnography, Critique.* Cambridge: Polity.

Hart, Keith. 2000. *The Memory Bank: Money in an Unequal world.* London: Profile Books.

Holbraad, Martin. 2005. "Expending Multiplicity: Money in Cuban Ifá Cults." *Journal of the Royal Anthropological Institute* 11 (2): 231–254.

Karlstrøm, Henrik. 2014. "Do Libertarians Dream of Electric Coins? The Material Embeddedness of Bitcoin." *Distinktion* 15 (1): 23–36.

Lave, Jean. 1988. *Cognition in Practice: Mind, Mathematics and Culture in Everyday Life.* Cambridge: Cambridge University Press.

Lazzer, Gian P. 2014. "Immigrants' Monetary Bank Practices: A Socialization Trajectory." *Italian Journal of Sociology of Education* 6 (3): 153–183.

Leach, Edmund. 1961. *Rethinking Anthropology.* London: Athlone Press.

Lévi-Strauss, Claude. 1954. "The Mathematics of Man." *International Social Science Bulletin* 6: 581–590.

MacKenzie, Donald, and Yuval Millo. 2003. "Constructing a Market, Performing Theory: The Historical Sociology of a Financial Derivatives Exchange." *American Journal of Sociology* 109 (1): 107–145.

Maurer, Bill. 2006. "The Anthropology of Money." *Annual Review of Anthropology* 35: 15–36.

Maurer, Bill. 2008. "Re-socialising Finance? Or Dressing It in Mufti? Calculating Alternatives for Cultural Economies." *Journal of Cultural Economy* 1 (1): 65–78.

Mauss, Marcel. (1925) 2007. *Essay sur le don.* Paris: Presses Universitaires de France.

Mimica, Jadran. 1988. *Intimations of Infinity: The Cultural Meanings of the Iqwaye Counting and Number Systems.* Oxford: Berg.

Mitchell, J. Clyde, ed. 1980. *Numerical Techniques in Social Anthropology.* Philadelphia, PA: Institute for the Study of Human Relationships.

Mosko, Mark S., and Frederick H. Damon, eds. 2005. *On the Order of Chaos: Social Anthropology and the Science of Chaos.* New York: Berghahn Books.

Parry, Jonathan, and Maurice Bloch, eds. 1989. *Money and the Morality of Exchange.* Cambridge: Cambridge University Press.

Passes, Alan. 2006. "From One to Metaphor: Toward an Understanding of Pa'ikwené (Palikur) Mathematics." *Tipití: Journal of the Society for the Anthropology of Lowland South America* 4 (1–2): 153–176.

Peebles, Gustav. 2002. "Money vs. Currency: A Response to W. Wolters." *Anthropology Today* 18 (1): 21–22.

Peebles, Gustav. 2012. "Filth and Lucre: The Dirty Money Complex as a Taxation Regime." *Anthropology Quarterly* 85 (4): 1229–1255.

Piaget, Jean. 1965. *The Child's Conception of Number.* Trans. Caleb Gattegno and F. M. Hodgson. New York: W. W. Norton.

Pickles, Anthony J. 2013. "Pocket Calculator: A Humdrum 'Obviator' in Papua New Guinea?" *Journal of the Royal Anthropological Institute* 19 (3): 510–526.

Polanyi, Karl. 1968. "The Semantics of Money-Uses." In *Primitive, Archaic, and Modern Economies: Essays of Karl Polanyi,* ed. George Dalton, 175–203. Boston: Beacon Press.

Rosin, R. Thomas. 1973. "Gold Medallions: The Arithmetic Calculations of an Illiterate." *Council on Anthropology and Education Newsletter* 4 (2): 1–9.

Ross, Sandy. 2014. "Virtual Money, Practices and Moral Orders in Second Life." *Distinktion* 15 (1): 6–22.

Rotman, Brian. 1993. *Ad Infinitum … The Ghost in Turing's Machine: Taking God Out of Mathematics and Putting the Body Back In*. Palo Alto, CA: Stanford University Press.

Saxe, Geoffrey B. 2012. *Cultural Development of Mathematical Ideas: The Papua New Guinea Studies*. New York: Cambridge University Press.

Simiand, François. 1932. *Le salaire, l'evolution sociale et la monnaie*. Paris: Alcan.

Simmel, Georg. (1907) 2011. *The Philosophy of Money*. Trans. Tom Bottomore and David Frisby. London: Routledge.

Strathern, Marilyn. 1992. "Qualified Value: The Perspective of Gift Exchange." In *Barter, Exchange and Value: An Anthropological Approach*, ed. Caroline Humphrey and Stephen Hugh-Jones, 169–191. Cambridge: Cambridge University Press.

Sun, John Z., Grace I. Wang, Vivek K. Goyal, and Lav R. Varshney. 2012. "A Framework for Bayesian Optimality of Psychophysical Laws." *Journal of Mathematical Psychology* 56 (6): 495–501.

Taussig, Michael T. 1980. *The Devil and Commodity Fetishism in South America*. Chapel Hill: University of North Carolina Press.

Urton, Gary, with Primitivo Nina Llanos. 1997. *The Social Life of Numbers: A Quechua Ontology of Numbers and Philosophy of Arithmetic*. Austin: University of Texas Press.

Verran, Helen. 2001. *Science and an African Logic*. Chicago: University of Chicago Press.

Verran, Helen. 2010. "Number as an Inventive Frontier in Knowing and Working Australia's Water Resources." *Anthropological Theory* 10 (1–2): 171–178.

Weber, Max. (1923) 1981. *General Economic History*. Trans. Frank H. Knight. New Brunswick, NJ: Transaction.

Weiss, Brad. 1997. "Northwestern Tanzania on a Single Shilling: Sociality, Embodiment, Valuation." *Cultural Anthropology* 12 (3): 335–361.

Yuran, Noam. 2014. *What Money Wants: An Economy of Desire*. Stanford, CA: Stanford University Press.

Zelizer, Viviana A. 1997. *The Social Meaning of Money: Pin Money, Paychecks, Poor Relief, and Other Currencies*. Princeton, NJ: Princeton University Press.

Chapter 1

# IS GOLD JEWELRY MONEY?

*Peter Oakley*

Saving your merry humour, here's the note.
How much your chain weighs to the utmost carat.

— *The Comedy of Errors*, Act IV, Scene 1

In November 2010, Robert Zoellick, the president of the World Bank, made a speech that caught economic journalists' attention. He proposed that policy makers should start to consider employing gold as "an international reference point" (Harding et al. 2010). At face value, Zoellick's comment was unsurprising. Policy makers needed to gauge consumer sentiment, and stating that the price of gold accurately reflected investor anxiety was not controversial. But having supported the 100-year-long project to try to wean the world off gold as money, the world's central bankers were less than enthusiastic to give the yellow metal a new role in international finance.

At the time Zoellick made this statement I was undertaking fieldwork on the fine jewelry industry and gold supply chains. The minor furor and

Notes for this chapter begin on page 28.

misinterpretations that followed his speech reinforced my observations that gold could inspire acute anxiety among bankers and traders. Fieldwork also offered numerous other insights into the uncomfortable relationship between gold and most of the world's fiat currencies. Gold's apparently unstoppable rise in value and respect had had dire consequences for the jewelry industry during my time in the field. In the course of the five years that I observed the sector, entire sections of the fine jewelry trade and precious metal refining industry were reconstructed by a rapidly changing social landscape.

Gold's capacity to undermine, as well as underpin, economic systems and even its own supply chains is not a recent development. The adoption of legally protected gold coinage, or specie, across medieval Europe brought with it intractable social problems particular to its materiality (see Bordo and Schwartz 1996; N. Clark 2014; Eichengreen and Flandreau 1985; Oakley 2013; Porteous 1973). These persisted until specie's fall from grace in the early twentieth century. Equally, in the contemporary world, gold continues to defy its reclassification as a classical commodity (Bernstein 2004; Blas and Mackintosh 2009; Green 1982; Hart 2013).

## The Consequences of Material Money

In the introduction to this book, Sandy Ross, Mario Schmidt, and Ville Koskinen note that despite their diverse material forms, different types of money are overwhelmingly treated as conceptually similar, somehow sharing an innate abstractive quality that negates material specificity. While acknowledging concerns that a focus on material qualities has too frequently led to unhelpful overemphasis on the immediate phenomenological properties of tokens of exchange (Holbraad 2005), the wider consequences of materiality still need to be considered in more depth. My continued adherence to this approach is due to the importance of material networks that make money exist as money. James Buchan (1997: 7) poetically reflects on using a Saudi Arabian riyal note to pay a Lebanese waiter: "The banknote was an outcrop of some vast mountain of social arrangements." Money exists as money only if it is facilitating these types of arrangements. Money as a total abstraction cannot actually be studied at all—only speculated on (Yuran 2014; Zelizer 1997).

Why is dwelling on this important? The material chosen to make money a concrete entity can have much wider social resonances. Although in the case of fiat currencies the leakage between the two identities is so limited as to be negligible—we do not see paper money and other pieces of paper as readily interchangeable—in the case of other types of money, particularly money made from precious metals, this incommensurability is less evident. This difference undermines the notion that we can simply extrapolate the experience of using a fiat currency to encompass all monetary relations.

The financial crisis of 2008 and subsequent sovereign debt crises exposed the specific mechanisms needed to maintain a fiat currency to an unprecedented degree and also emboldened the critics of these types of currency systems (e.g.,

Eisen 2012; Harding et al. 2010; Mattingly and Schmidt 2010). In the United States, a vocal section of the political right has consistently advocated a return to a precious metal based coinage, which it claims would inevitably engender a return to fiscal prudence (Lewis 2007). Yet the alternative monetary tokens created to facilitate this shift, such as silver 'liberty' dollars, have repeatedly fallen prey to compromising scams. These events expose the astounding naiveté on the part of actors regarding how currency systems rely for their continued existence on governmental power, rather than common goodwill or the 'invisible hand' of the free market.

The fundamental risk faced by monetary economies based on precious metal coinage has always been the material coin itself. Problems that can arise include a crisis of trust in authenticity or face value, the overall supply, or a sudden decline in the velocity of circulation. Sometimes these factors combine, with each reinforcing the effects of the others. Regional or even national financial breakdowns caused by a lack of specie in circulation were once endemic (Clay and Tungate 2009; Eichengreen and Flandreau 1985; Levenson 2009). Social disruptions from war to crop failure could lead to a 'run on the banks', when a large percentage of the population would fight—sometimes literally—to convert wealth from paper derivatives, such as promissory notes, into gold coins, which were then hoarded (Bernstein 2004). Economic collapse could also be precipitated by a sequence of events unimaginable in a fiat system. In 1857, the steamer SS *Central America* was lost in a hurricane in the Gulf of Mexico. As the ship was carrying stocks of gold to replenish the coinage desperately needed by US East Coast cities, news of the disaster led to financial panic (Kinder 1998; Klare 1991).

Although more restricted than a medium of exchange that relies on immediate claims of value, such as salt (Godelier 1971) or grain (Fuller 1989), specie is more intrinsically international than a fiat currency. The gold content in the specie of one nation or empire enables it to operate as a para-currency in all others that adhere to a gold standard. Specie's material basis also offers potentials not available to fiat currencies. In a fiat system, the lowest denomination coin is the practical limit case of divisibility for direct exchange, and the value of every token is immutable. Stock market trades may be conducted at small fractions of the smallest unit of the currency, but these can only be redeemed once aggregated to a workable level. In contrast, each individual piece of specie holds the potential of apparent boundless divisibility. In practice, gold coins could be, and often were, cut in half or further subdivided and then used for trade (Porteous 1973). While these divided coins were no longer sanctioned currency, at times they took on an important role in the money supply.

The material nature of specie resulted in specific day-to-day anxieties and behaviors. Trading was accompanied by continual checking to ensure that each gold coin being proffered was not a forgery and contained sufficient gold. Delicate miniature beam or cantilever balances made specifically to test specie were an essential possession of every banker and trader. Reconfirming the material validity of tokens of exchange became a ritual element of trading, defining not only the speed of trade and the behavior of participants, but also their expectations of how trade should be conducted as a performative act. Today, the process of weighing coins has been 'black boxed' by technologies to the extent that we barely perceive it unless a machine summarily rejects our money. Our confusion in such situations—is this a fault in the machine or is the coin somehow sub-standard or fake?—illustrates how little we are aware of what the coins we use should feel like. In a specie-based economy, the immediate physical qualities of precious metals cannot be partitioned off from the way the entire economic system is structured and functions. To take Marshall McLuhan's ([1964] 2001) axiom in a new direction, in the case of specie, the medium really is the message.

## Defining Jewelry

While specie is overwhelmingly considered to be a functional financial instrument, jewelry is typically framed as a personal valuable primarily intended for social display. This position informs popular notions as well as anthropological and sociological academic discourse (Bourdieu [1984] 2008; Goffman 1951; Simmel 1997; Weiner 1992). In practice, the multivalent identity of gold jewelry enables it to undertake other types of social work, although these are usually elided or left purposefully indistinct. To uncover them, we will start with an examination of what the word 'jewelry' actually refers to in practice, and then move on to consider a historic type of jewelry that challenges common-sense descriptions. We will conclude with an analysis of recent events which show that even contemporary gold jewelry is treated by individuals as an object type much closer to money than is generally acknowledged.

In academic contexts, the terms 'jewelry' and 'personal adornment' are often used interchangeably, which poses problems for historians of art and design and anthropologists alike when they attempt to categorize things that people drape, tie, bind, or push through parts of their body, either using pre-existing protrusions, cavities, or holes, or making new ones expressly for the purpose. Yet the general understanding of the English word 'jewelry' is much more restricted in daily use. Most Westerners accept that others may use dog's teeth, feathers, or nuts for adornment and will admire the results when these are exhibited within the confines of ethnographic collections. But they have no intention of wearing such things themselves. The range of materials that can be used to make high-status jewelry is actually very narrow, highly stable, and easily identifiable: gold, platinum, silver, and the 'big five' gems (diamonds, rubies, sapphires, emeralds, and pearls). This convention has a very long history in Europe and elsewhere (G. Clark 1986; Cocks 1980; Forsyth 2013).

Three descriptive labels widely used in the jewelry trade—fine jewelry, costume jewelry, and fashion jewelry (Event Guides 2011; Goldsmiths 2011; Reed Exhibitions 2011)—illustrate this neatly. Fine jewelry is made from the historically sanctioned expensive materials. Costume jewelry formally copies fine jewelry but falls short in terms of its materials. Fashion jewelry is formally eclectic, low value, and disposable. It is as impossible to make fashion jewelry from gold and diamonds as it is to make fine jewelry from plastic and hemp. Gold jewelry is understood to be fine jewelry, and the higher the gold content of the gold alloy, the better. Although artisanship has some role in appraisal, the materials still make the object what it is. This is a strange situation. Object categories are not generally materially constrained. For example, a chair is still a chair, whether it is made of wood, metal, or glass.[1]

## Money Chains

Although these two classes of objects—specie and jewelry—are generally considered to have very different social roles, there is evidence that conceptual confluence exists in practice. This can best be illustrated by examining the social identity of a specific type of jewelry that was popular for more than 100 years: the money chain. Wearing elaborate gold collars or chains made of decorated links was a common practice among European nobility and senior officials in the late Middle Ages and the Renaissance. Effigies on the tomb of Philip the Handsome and Juana la Loca, carved in 1519 and 1520, represent them both wearing such collars (Muller 1972). Extant paintings show, and contemporary documents describe, the familial or personal emblems represented on each link. These designs also featured on the chains-of-office of senior retainers. John of Gaunt (1340–1399), his son Henry IV of England, and his nephew Richard II of England all used the double-S symbol, which was revived by the founder of the Tudor dynasty, Henry VII (1457–1509) and eventually became the badge of office of the entire English royal household (Evans [1953] 1970).

By the sixteenth century, a fashion had developed for also wearing heavier chains with simple 'O' shaped links. Portraits from the early and mid-1500s provide ample evidence of this practice. Examples from the northern states of Europe include Strigel's portrait of Hieronymus Haller (1503) and the infamous Holbein portrait of Anne of Cleeves (1539). That Anne chose to be depicted wearing such chains for a portrait intended to enchant a future royal husband indicates the allure of these objects to contemporary viewers of the painting.

Simple gold chains were also adopted as personal adornment lower down the social scale. Rich German townswomen increasingly displayed their wealth by the number of simple gold chains they wore (Lightbrown 1992). That gold jewelry had become popular elsewhere among the general populace is evidenced by an exchange between the Silesian knight Nicholas von Popilievo and an inhabitant of Seville. Outraged at being asked if he is a knight, Von Popilievo replies: "Can you not see the ensigns of a knight hung around my neck? Know that in my country it is not a custom for pagans, Jews and rustics to adorn themselves with gold as they do in yours: Only knights may do this" (quoted in ibid.: 241). Von Popilievo's outburst indicates the extent to which Spain's recent conquests in the New World, and the resulting influx of gold, had led to innovations in adornment.

In 1980, the remains of the Spanish treasure ship *Santa Margarita* were discovered off the Florida Keys. The *Santa Margarita* sank in a hurricane in 1622, a century after simple gold chains had become popular in Europe, but finds from the wreck proved that they were still fashionable. The recovery of more than 50 money chains confirmed a consistent feature of these objects that had been suspected from previous examinations of the few remaining scattered examples: each link in a money chain weighed exactly an ounce (Shaughnessy 2004). This regularity was no coincidence. The gold links weighed the same as a contemporary Spanish eight escudo gold coin. If pressed for cash, a wearer could simply remove a link from the chain and use it as payment. The malleability of high-carat gold alloys made this action possible without recourse to specialist equipment. A money chain therefore came as close to being interchangeable with contemporary currency as it was possible for a non-specie object to be.

The ostentation of the money chain interacted with the practicality of its use as a means of payment. The simplicity of each of the links was more than just an aesthetic choice; their form made it relatively easy to determine the weight and specific gravity of the link. As these were needed to complete a comprehensive gold assay, the form of the money chain facilitated its functionality as an object of exchange. In the money chain we find a piece of jewelry that exhibits the same properties as money in terms of recursive divisibility. The chain is a conceptual whole made up of many subsidiary but equally recognizable and potentially independent wholes. It is also partible: once a link is removed, the owner retains the original chain and 'gains' an additional object, the single link. The extent to which a money chain can repeatedly relinquish links and still retain conceptually integrity does have a limit, much like the sorites paradox.[2] But it is worth noting that money chains were far longer than the gold chains that are worn today. One of the money chains found in the wreck of the *Santa Maria* was over three meters in length.

The simplicity of the money chain had another aspect—formal anonymity—that also supported its use as an object of exchange. Whereas the heraldic imagery of emblematic collars restricted their circulation to related individuals and their servants, a simple gold chain could be worn by anyone. Thus, a money chain could potentially circulate with spectacular velocity, taking one of many alternative possible pathways. As well as gifts of esteem or parts of dowries, money chains were used as bribes or rewards for political services rendered. Henry VIII of England was not above requisitioning a chain from one courtier to give to another as a reward for a favor (Lightbrown 1992). Their obvious value and anonymity led to a role in international relations. The convention arose of giving foreign ambassadors a plain gold chain as a parting present (Cappellieri 2018; Hackett 2015). When the Republic of Venice decided that returning ambassadors had to surrender these gifts to the city-state's treasury, it led to passionate, although unsuccessful, petitions from the Republic's aggrieved statesmen.

The money chain's ability to announce wealth but not origins was not lost on contemporary social commentators. Shakespeare makes use of the money chain's obvious value and subtle ambiguities in *The Comedy of Errors*, first performed in 1604. The action takes place in Ephesus, a town where trade and profit are paramount and personal relationships are frequently compromised by the urge for material gain. The plot, which hinges on mounting confusion surrounding the identities of two pairs of identical twins, relies in part on a sequence of misunderstandings over a substantial gold chain. The action and moral message of Shakespeare's dark comedy relies on the multiplicity of social pathways open to such an object. Originally intended as a gift for a wife, the gold chain is mistakenly given to and worn by one of the twins, then coveted by a courtesan. The chain's lack of any secure position or clear identity mirrors that of the play's main protagonists. It is worth noting that in order for events of the play to be understood, the ambiguity of the gold chain had to be obvious to contemporary audiences. *The Comedy of Errors* illustrates not only that the money chain as object type mediated a diverse range of relationships and interactions in Renaissance Europe, but also that the money chain's social liquidity led to a measure of disquiet and critical comment.

Should we see the money chain as simply a type of money? I would contend it is more interesting than that. Money chains were socially ambiguous and thus a suitable means of rewarding individuals in situations where an overt payment made using something accepted as money would be considered either crass or socially reprehensible. It is the very ambiguity of the money chain as an object—directly comparable with money, but not quite money—that made it a suitable political gift, component of a dowry, or present to a courtesan. Its precise value could be both closely calculated and ostensibly ignored.

## Researching Jewelry in a Time of Economic Crisis

Are money chains a historic anomaly? Or are they a type of gold jewelry that makes an inherent aspect of jewelry become more obvious? The money chain as an object form has no direct correlation with the predominant types of jewelry offered for sale today by most high street jewelers in Britain. The closest object is the rapper chain, worn by some hip hop music enthusiasts. But these objects are usually made from gold alloys with a far lower gold content, making them ersatz copies rather than modern equivalents of the money chain. Most other typical forms of jewelry are far more delicate in construction and lighter in weight, with design and artisanship rather than weight as the overriding factor in their appeal and an apparently significant factor in their initial retail price. However, these differences mask an underlying similarity that becomes apparent only at specific moments in each piece of jewelry's later social trajectory.

Observing these moments is not easy, although during my fieldwork in the jewelry industry, exceptional circumstances made them more frequent and numerous. The year 2008 saw the start of a long-running economic crisis that led to a flight to safe financial instruments, and, as a consequence, the gold price rose continuously for more than four years (CPM Group 2014; O'Connell et al. 2013). Although the 2008–2012 climb in the gold price was unprecedented, fieldwork interviews with industry professionals revealed that this instability was a chronic rather than acute feature of the jewelry industry. Respondents described previous sudden climbs and crashes in the gold price. These included a major spike in the early 1980s that resulted in a 'gold rush' in London's jewelry district, with queues of people stretching down the street waiting to sell their gold jewelry at the refiners' commercial trade counters.

In contrast, the length and consistency of the rise in the gold price between 2008 and 2012 presented an opportunity for alternative 'scrap gold' purchasers to set up businesses in competition with established pawnbrokers and industrial trade counters. The industry also witnessed the arrival of postal gold companies that bought gold items sent through the mail. During 2010, magazines and UK daytime television were saturated with advertisements encouraging the public to sell unwanted gold jewelry (English 2012; Saner 2012). These purchasers became known collectively as 'cash-for-gold' businesses. In 2013, stagnating gold prices, the decline in sources of easily available scrap, and increasing concerns about the low prices being paid by many cash-for-gold companies caused the collapse of the cash-for-gold market. By 2015, the number of scrap purchasers had returned to something approaching the same size as before the boom.

My participant-observation activities as an assayer and refinery worker revealed the hidden side of these cash-for-gold operations: staggering amounts of gold jewelry that was purchased and processed as scrap. Thousands of kilos of jewelry were melted down to make gold 'melt bars' that were sold to the large refiners to be turned into gold bullion, which was then sold on the international exchanges (see CPM Group 2014; O'Connell et al. 2013). At field sites, any interest in the composition of the trays full of jewelry, called musters, waiting to be melted down was not encouraged, and I was repeatedly warned not to inspect these tangled piles of jewelry. The convention was to treat the musters as undifferentiated raw material rather than a collection of discrete objects. From conversations with refinery staff, I discovered that this overt denial of the 'objectness' of the jewelry in front of them was learned behavior. When asked if he ever thought about the jewelry he destroyed each day, one respondent told me: "Well, I did at first, but now it all just sort of passes in front of me. It's a bit depressing to even go there."

Musters were predominantly composed of two types of jewelry. The first was small nondescript items: thin chains, earrings, and pendants that could have been made any time over the past half-century. The second was larger and heavier unfashionable objects that could be fairly closely dated on stylistic grounds. Examples were 'gypsy bangles', Dunhill lighters, charm bracelets, and ingot pendants, all of which were popular in the 1970s and early 1980s. When tactfully prompted, it turned out that furnace operators were fully aware of the nature of the jewelry they were destroying. They could even describe trends in the appearance and disappearance of different types of items. One worker explained that gypsy bangles, which had been extremely popular in the 1970s and 1980s, were now too dated to be resold by jewelers or pawnbrokers as jewelry but fetched a good price when sold as scrap due to their relatively high weight. The same applied to gold Dunhill lighters, which had become less resalable because of long-term decline in smoking and associated public rituals, such as lighting someone else's cigarette. Referring to the extremely nondescript items, one furnace operator remarked that he was "gradually destroying all the crap Ratner had made a fortune selling in the 80s." This was an astute reference to Gerald Ratner's well-known chain of jewelry stores that had sold huge volumes of cut-price 9 carat jewelry during the 1980s. The company had almost gone bankrupt in 1991 after Ratner made an ill-advised speech at a Confederation of British Industry (CBI) dinner, boasting that his products were poorly made rubbish (IOD 2013; Ratner 2007).

The pieces of gold jewelry that predominated in the musters were middling in both value and aesthetics. While holding enough value as stores of gold to be worth the effort of taking them to be scrapped, they were not valuable enough or aesthetically significant enough to be cherished as status symbols. It was this combination of material and formal mediocrity, together with the underlying value of their material composition, which led to their eventual assimilation into the muster. In contrast to the recursive divisibility of the money chain, the muster was conventionally treated by handlers as an indivisible conceptual entity, despite their knowledge that it consisted of a multiplicity of individual objects. This conceptualization, demanded by the context of its assembly as a muster, foreshadowed the physical unification of the gold jewelry into the form of the melt bar. However, this was not the case for other, far longer-lived private assemblages: jewelry collections.

## The Jewelry Collection as a Meta-Object

It was fieldwork among retail sales staff that provided crucial insights into the nature of the jewelry collection as a meta-object, as well as the earlier trajectories of objects that constituted the major part of refinery musters. As a result of their work with extraordinary pieces, art and design historians, museum curators, conservators, and auction house appraisers all display a marked tendency to consider gold jewelry as singularities and to emphasize rare or unique features (e.g., Bury 1984; G. Clark 1986; Dormer and Turner 1985; Orrling 2002). In fairness, the individuality of the items they deal with strongly supports this approach. But this perception of jewelry contrasts with that of shop assistants on high streets in Britain. They, and many of their clients, considered jewelry in more relative terms. These consumers owned a jewelry collection that existed as a fluid meta-object containing a number of visually and materially related items.

Jewelry collections were usually the outcome of a sequence of purchases that had taken place over years. In jewelry stores, consumers would deliberate over new purchases, reflecting on whether a potential addition would 'go with' (i.e., neither aesthetically clash nor formally duplicate) the pieces they already owned. As different colored metals do not visually complement each other, gold owners were future gold buyers. Once established as collections, these assemblages held the capacity to expand indefinitely, being limited only by the availability of suitable items and the financial resources of the owner. A jewelry collection could also contract or change some of its individual constituent pieces at any point without suffering conceptual dissolution. Jewelry that became unfashionable was increasingly at risk of being 'dropped', a decision that would lead to its appearance in a muster at a future point. The owners of jewelry collections almost invariably possessed individual items of high symbolic or sentimental value, such as engagement or wedding rings. These would be understood to be on a different register and were treated as distinct from the collection, although they usually aligned with it to some degree in terms of visual aesthetics and material composition.

A jewelry collection as a whole reflects the changing financial status and personal taste of the owner. Its fluidity is critical to its longevity as a meta-object. While similar inward flows are common to all collections of objects, controlled outflows are generally much more problematic to maintain. In the case of gold jewelry, this was achieved in large measure by a unique feature of jewelry made using precious metals: the hallmark. In Britain, it is a legal requirement that any object offered for sale that is claimed to be made of gold—with the exception of extremely small items or medical or scientific equipment—must have a hallmark that has been applied at one of the four registered Assay Offices. A hallmark identifies the percentage of gold in the alloy the item is made of, as well as where it was marked and who submitted the item for marking. As Britain is a signatory to the international treaty known as the Precious Metals Convention, gold objects bearing similar assay marks from other signatory countries are also legally acceptable in Britain.[3] The existence and ubiquity of the hallmark means that anyone handling a piece of hallmarked jewelry can quickly and reliably calculate the amount of gold that it contains.

This hallmarking system allowed cash-for-gold businesses to give immediate scrap valuations for gold objects presented to them and allowed owners to calculate how close the offer was to the day's spot price for gold. Hallmarks are also a guarantee against fraud, due to the Assay Offices' expertise, the government's protective legislation, and active policing policies. Consequently, the hallmarking system facilitates both the commodification and destruction of gold jewelry. By offering a guarantee of the gold content, it increases the liquidity of gold jewelry in general and the fluidity of every jewelry collection in the United Kingdom.

The jewelry collection as a meta-object exhibits the same recursive divisibility as the money chain or the heap of gold coins. In contrast to the coins, whose liquidity was determined by their status as a legal, material token of exchange, and the money chain, whose liquidity was facilitated by the form of its constituent links, the liquidity of the jewelry collection is facilitated by the existence of the hallmarking system. This permits individual pieces of gold jewelry items to be highly variable in terms of form, weight, and composition because a scrap buyer can still easily and confidently determine the overall gold content by weighing the item and making a simple calculation using the information embedded in the hallmark.

## Jewelry as Money?

This leads us to some final key questions. Martin Holbraad (2005) argues that money is uniquely divisible, with an exceptional capacity for displacement. But we have seen in the examples above that particular types of gold jewelry, and some aggregations of gold jewelry, exhibit the same properties. There are two possible conclusions to consider. Either money is less exceptional than claimed, or gold jewelry is actually a type of money, although not recognized as such. I should add a couple of caveats here, as they will help us take the last steps. Not all gold jewelry carries the same capacity for circulation. We have already noted that some object forms, including the heraldic collar, engagement ring, and wedding ring, are just too individual to circulate with any great velocity (English 2012; Saner 2012). We could list other, similarly exceptional items, such as royal regalia, Fabergé eggs, and Bronze Age torcs. The key word here is exceptional: the more mediocre or unremarkable an object becomes, the more likely it is to circulate unimpeded, with its material content determining the upper limit of its value.

So how much anonymous jewelry actually exists? As I mentioned earlier, the amounts only start to become apparent when one sees the musters of gold on the refiner's shop floor. The exceptional pieces of gold jewelry, from crowns to torcs, really are the exception in terms of overall weight of gold being used. In 2009, the UK's jewelry industry used 325,000 troy ounces (just over 10 metric tons) of gold to make jewelry, according to market analysts CPM Group (2014). This was also the first year in over a decade that more gold jewelry was scrapped in the United Kingdom than fabricated (Flood 2010). But as previously noted, this figure was a low point for industrial gold jewelry fabrication. In 2001, the UK jewelry industry needed 1,185,000 troy ounces of gold, almost 37 metric tons. In the same year, overall commercial jewelry manufacture across Europe accounted for 23,375,000 troy ounces, just more than 737 metric tons (CPM Group 2014), while the Italian gold jewelry industry alone, which specializes in mass producing standard chains (Green 1968), used 16,900,000 troy ounces, more than 525 metric tons (CPM Group 2014). Despite these large figures, we must acknowledge that the aggregated objects discussed here are far more limited than most types of money. As a microcosm, a single link is a far larger element of the macrocosm of the money chain than a single currency token is of an entire currency. In addition, it was the link's direct comparability to the contemporary units of currency in terms of overall weight and material composition that enabled the owner to make an accurate evaluation of its value. Taking this into account, the money chain should be considered a type of para-money rather than money proper.

Equally, when considering the value of the masses of unremarkable jewelry that constitute most jewelry collections in the United Kingdom, one has to recognize how much smaller the overall amounts are in relation to the UK's legally backed currency, as well as the restricted opportunities for conversion. Despite high levels of competition at the height of the cash-for-gold boom, even then the points of exchange were far more limited than the opportunities to realize the value of British pounds and pence. In addition, in every one of these situations, the value of the jewelry in question could be realized only through being converted into the national fiat currency. So while gold jewelry acts as a store of wealth, it remains less liquid than, and comparable only through, the legally sanctioned fiat currency. The jewelry collection exists as a type of para-money, rather than an independent or even stand-alone monetary system.

That said, I would contend that as well as being less than 'full' money, gold jewelry is also something more. With regard to the money chain, it was precisely the ambiguity of the object that allowed it to be used as a mediator in especially sensitive situations. For the modern jewelry collection, this is equally the case. It is the lack of any confirmed monetary status of gold jewelry, as well as its recognizable value, that makes it such an appropriate gift at these moments. In situations where offering an acknowledged currency would be considered too uncouth or mercenary, and where appearances or at least reasonable doubt needs to be maintained, gold jewelry remains the most appropriate token of exchange.

## Acknowledgments

The fieldwork that underpins much of this chapter was made possible due to an Arts and Humanities Research Council (AHRC) Doctoral Training Award. I would like to express my gratitude for this support, as well as the time and information shared by respondents in the field and the commercial organizations that permitted me access to their highly restricted sites and activities.

---

**Peter Oakley** is a Reader in Material Culture in the School of Arts and Humanities at the Royal College of Art in London. His research interests include the social identities of prestige materials and luxury goods, the introduction and retention of manufacturing techniques and processes, ethical material sourcing initiatives and certification programs, and the social impact of material standards and related analytical techniques. He is a Fellow of the Royal Anthropological Institute, an Honorary Research Fellow at University College London, and an Associate Member of the Winchester Luxury Research Group.

## Notes

1. For a review of object categorizations, see Margolis and Laurence (2007).
2. See the discussions about recursive divisibility and the sorites paradox in the introduction to this book.
3. See "Hallmarking Act 1973," Her Majesty's Government, National Archives, http://www.legislation.gov.uk/ukpga/1973/43.

# References

Bernstein, Peter L. 2004. *The Power of Gold: The History of an Obsession*. Chichester: John Wiley & Sons.

Blas, Javier, and James Mackintosh. 2009. "Hedge Fund Offers to Price Shares in Gold." *Financial Times*, 29 January. https://www.ft.com/content/efe1a910-ed98 -11dd-bd60-0000779fd2ac.

Bordo, Michael D., and Anna J. Schwartz. 1996. "The Operation of the Specie Standard: Evidence for Core and Peripheral Countries, 1880–1990." In *Currency Convertibility: The Gold Standard and Beyond*, ed. Jorge Braga de Macedo, Barry Eichengreen, and Jaime Reis, 85–100. London: Routledge.

Bourdieu, Pierre. (1984) 2008. *Distinction: A Social Critique of the Judgement of Taste*. Trans. Richard Nice. London: Routledge & Kegan Paul.

Buchan, James. 1997. *Frozen Desire: An Inquiry into the Meaning of Money*. New York: Farrar, Straus and Giroux.

Bury, Shirley. 1984. *An Introduction to Rings*. London: Her Majesty's Stationery Office.

Cappellieri, Alba. 2018. *Catene: Gioelli fra storia, funzione e ornamento* [Chains: Jewellery in history, function and ornament]. Milan: Silvana Editoriale.

Clark, Grahame. 1986. *Symbols of Excellence: Precious Materials as Expressions of Status*. Cambridge: Cambridge University Press.

Clark, Neil D. L. 2014. *Scottish Gold: Fruit of the Nation*. Castle Douglas: Neil Wilson.

Clay, Richard, and Sue Tungate, eds. 2009. *Matthew Boulton and the Art of Making Money*. Studley: Brewin Books.

Cocks, Anna S. 1980. *An Introduction to Courtly Jewellery*. London: Pitman Publishing.

CPM Group. 2014. *The CPM Gold Yearbook 2014*. London: Euromoney.

Dormer, Peter, and Ralph Turner. 1985. *The New Jewelry: Trends and Traditions*. London: Thames & Hudson.

Eichengreen, Barry, and Marc Flandreau, eds. 1985. *The Gold Standard in Theory and History*. London: Methuen.

Eisen, Sarah, ed. 2012. *Currencies After the Crash: The Uncertain Future of the Global Paper-Based Currency System*. New York: McGraw-Hill.

English, Simon. 2012. "Good for Barry, but Rise of Pawnbroking's Still a Worry." *Evening Standard*, 21 February. http://www.standard.co.uk/business/markets/good-for-barry-but-rise-of-pawnbrokings-still-a-worry-7445419.html.

Evans, Joan. (1953) 1970. *A History of Jewelry: 1100–1870*. London: Faber & Faber.

Event Guides. 2011. *The Jewelry Show Official Show Catalogue*. Carlisle: Event Guides Ltd.

Flood, Chris. 2010. "Investors Outshone Jewellery Buyers in Gold Rush of 2009." *Financial Times*, 14 January.

Forsyth, Hazel. 2013. *London's Lost Jewels: The Cheapside Hoard*. London: I. B. Tauris.

Fuller, Christopher J. 1989 "Misconceiving the Grain Heap: A Critique of the Concept of the Indian Jajmani System." In *Money and the Morality of Exchange*, ed. Jonathan Parry and Maurice Bloch, 33–63. Cambridge: Cambridge University Press.

Godelier, Maurice. 1971. "'Salt Currency' and the Circulation of Commodities among the Baruya of New Guinea." In *Studies in Economic Anthropology*, ed. George Dalton, 52–73. Washington, DC: American Anthropological Association.

Goffman, Erving. 1951. "Symbols of Class Status." *British Journal of Sociology* 2 (4): 294–304.

Goldsmiths. 2011. *Goldsmiths Fair '11*. London: Goldsmiths Company.

Green, Timothy. 1968. *The World of Gold*. London: Michael Joseph.

Green, Timothy. 1982. *The New World of Gold: The Inside Story of the Mines, the Markets, the Politics, the Investors*. London: Weidenfield & Nicolson.

Hackett, Helen. 2015. *Early Modern Exchanges: Dialogues between Nations and Cultures, 1550–1750*. Farnham: Ashgate.

Harding, Robin, Javier Blas, and Alan Beattie. 2010. "World Economy: In Gold They Rush." *Financial Times*, 12 November. https://www.ft.com/content/d77d01f8-ee90 -11df-9db0-00144feab49a.

Hart, Matthew. 2013. *Gold: The Race for the World's Most Seductive Metal*. London: Simon & Schuster.

Holbraad, Martin. 2005. "Expending Multiplicity: Money in Cuban Ifá Cults." *Journal of the Royal Anthropological Institute* 11 (2): 231–254.

IOD (Institute of Directors). 2013. "Gerald Ratner Speaking at the 1991 Institute of Directors Annual Convention." YouTube, 3 May. https://www.youtube.com/ watch?v=Nj9BZz71yQE.

Kinder, Gary. 1998. *Ship of Gold in the Deep Blue Sea*. London: Little, Brown.

Klare, Normand E. 1991. *The Final Voyage of* Central America, *1857: The Saga of a Gold Rush Steamship, the Tragedy of Her Loss in a Hurricane, and the Treasure Which Is Now Recovered*. Glendale: Arthur H. Clark.

Levenson, Thomas. 2009. *Newton and the Counterfeiter: The Unknown Detective Career of the World's Greatest Scientist*. London: Faber & Faber.

Lewis, Nathan. 2007. *Gold: The Once and Future Money*. Hoboken, NJ: John Wiley & Sons.

Lightbrown, Ronald W. 1992. *Medieval European Jewellery*. London: Victoria and Albert Publications.

Margolis, Eric, and Stephen Laurence, eds. 2007. *Creations of the Mind: Theories of Artifacts and Their Representation*. Oxford: Oxford University Press.

Mattingly, Phil, and Robert Schmidt. 2010. "Ron Paul's Moment." *Bloomberg Business-week*, 6–12 December.

McLuhan, Marshall. (1964). 2001. *Understanding Media*. London: Routledge.

Muller, Priscilla E. 1972. *Jewels in Spain: 1500–1800*. New York: Hispanic Society of America.

Oakley, Peter. 2013. "Containing Precious Metals: Hallmarking, Minting and the Mate-riality of Gold and Silver in Medieval and Modern England." In *Mobility, Meaning and Transformations of Things: Shifting Contexts of Material Culture through Time*, ed. Hans Peter Hahn and Hadas Weiss, 63–77. Oxford: Oxbow Books.

O'Connell, Rhona, Cameron Alexander, Andrew Leyland et al. 2013. *Gold Survey 2013 Update 1*. London: Thomson Reuters GFMS. http://share.thomsonreuters.com/PR/ Misc/GFMS/GoldSurvey2013Update1.pdf.

Orrling, Carin. 2002. *The Gold Room*. Stockholm: Statens Historiska Museum.

Porteous, John. 1973. *Coins*. London: Octopus Books.

Ratner, Gerald. 2007. *The Rise and Fall … and Rise Again*. Chichester: Capstone.

Reed Exhibitions. 2011. *International Jewellery London 2011 Essential Guide*. London: Publishing Events.

Saner, Emine. 2012. "Gold Fever." *G2*, 1 February.

Shaughnessy, Carol. 2004. *Diving into Glory: The Mel Fisher Maritime Museum*. Key West, FL: Mel Fisher Maritime Heritage Society.

Simmel, Georg. 1997. "Adornment." In *Simmel on Culture: Selected Writings*, ed. David Frisby and Mike Featherstone, 206–211. London: Sage.

Weiner, Annette B. 1992. *Inalienable Possessions: The Paradox of Keeping-While-Giving*. Berkeley: University of California Press.

Yuran, Noam. 2014. *What Money Wants: An Economy of Desire*. Stanford, CA: Stanford University Press.

Zelizer, Viviana A. 1997. *The Social Meaning of Money: Pin Money, Paychecks, Poor Relief, and Other Currencies*. Princeton, NJ: Princeton University Press.

# Chapter 2

# INJURY AND MEASUREMENT
Jacob Grimm on Blood Money and
Concrete Quantification

*Anna Echterhölter*

Theodore Porter (1995: ix) describes quantification as a language "well suited for communication that goes beyond the boundaries of locality and community." Although historical reflections on this new communication structure are still scarce, work on historical epistemology of economic practices is emerging (Dommann et al. 2014). Studies engaging critically with infrastructures (Schabacher 2013: 138) and state administration (Scott 1998: 31) frequently identify metrology and the establishment of weights and measures as crucial to political economy. This chapter explores the onset of metrical infrastructures as they can be reconstructed from rural law decrees. There are two modes of non-numerical quantification—material property and monetary value—through Jacob Grimm's accounts of early German laws. While his juridical studies have received ample recognition (Renner 2012; Schmidt-Wiegand 1999; Wyss 1979), their metrological core remains under-studied. Grimm approaches the monetary sphere in a remarkably procedural way. In the rural settings he investigates, measures are primarily needed to determine field boundaries, usage rights, amounts of material, probable yields, and workforce performance standards. Property borders and a concrete, procedural notion of ownership are of key concern. For example, whoever neglects his or her land, such that it risks becoming overgrown, loses it to the village community. The criterion of measurement for this is when "two oxen will lose sight of each other in the new forest" (Grimm [1828] 1992: 128).[1] In a more industrialized setting, such matters would be resolved by contracts indicating precise monetary sums. But these agreements would be meaningless if the units of measurement were not clearly indicated therein.

Metrology, or measurement, connects money's referentiality to concrete materialities. This is why local forms of economic measurement are revealing for any investigation of money, and even more so when the quality of quantification is a key concern (Engster 2014; Kula 1986). Drawing on studies of cultural techniques of numeracy (Maye 2010; Verran 2010; Wedell 2004), this analysis discusses differences between Grimm's procedural measurements and the findings of scientific histories of quantification (Frängsmyr et al. 1990; Schaffer 1997, 2000; Wise 1995), including explicitly practice-oriented studies (Alder 1998; Gooday 2004; Schaffer 2015; Schlaudt 2009; Sibum 1998). The first part of this chapter outlines the quantification procedures explained in Grimm's work on Germanic law. The second part considers the particular case of measuring value.

The procedures that Grimm calls 'measurements' are functionally analogous to standard measures, but do not produce the same precision and exactitude. They differ from the multiplicity of value scales that Guyer (2004: 49) observes in West African economic history. In these regions, a range of measuring scales is more readily available for calculating transactions. But even using intervals, or socially invested, value-laden rankings, still involves numerical operations. Grimm instead suggests thinking about measurement in a non-numerical way. Qualities of things—their sizes, sounds, colors, and reflective properties—can be used. For example, one may navigate a lake as far as a red shield can be seen on the shore (Grimm [1828] 1992: 104). It is the explicit imprecision and ambiguity of these measures that turns them into promising research objects, especially when measuring property (Ross 2013). Grimm's examples are at odds with scientific conceptions of measurement, particularly because numeracy is not required. If numbers appear, they are woven into symbolic actions as it is believed that they may invite chance or fate.

The second part of the chapter focuses on value measurement, which is still considered a key function of money (Dodd 2005: 409). Grimm uses examples from European blood money traditions that involve the wergild value system. During the Early Middle Ages, wergild (or 'man price') is mentioned in all major law codices and is considered a likely mechanism for the development of monetary institutions. Since the 1960s, publications on special purpose monies (e.g., Dalton 1965; Polanyi 1977) have historicized separate functions of money that were in use before coins. Guyer (2011) encourages investigation in the separate functions of money, but objects to such evolutionary trajectories.

Instead, she analyzes the local interplay of multiple currencies, decentralizing the dominant function of the 'medium of exchange'. Grimm does not treat money separately, but his engagement with measures constitutes a vital contribution to such readings. He follows money's function 'backwards' into rural regions, where coins and precise numbers are not widely used. Whether through amounts or values, quantification emerges in his studies as a category that is quite different from its representation as the agent of commensuration, enlightenment, and hyper-modernity.

## Procedural Measurement: Ambiguity and Negotiation

The question of quantification recurs in historical rural law codes that Jacob Grimm collected, commented on, and published as *Weisthümer* ([1840–1878] 2000). He quotes from a farmers' field cooperative code, or *Markgenossenschaft*, communal rules that limit when wood can be cut: "It is further our ancient law and our old freewill that a *Markgenosse* on this side of the river is not allowed to hew any oak or beech wood that is still so green that a hawk likes to eat beneath it in mid summer" (cited in Schoof 1953: 230). Crucial amounts are created by minute descriptions. Everything depends on the leaves: their shadow's expansion gives an approximate size in relation to the hawk's body. Thus, the codes form a rough measure in keeping with changing seasons and plant growth. Grimm extols the poetry of this passage: "How beautifully is the size of the branch—which is forbidden to be cut down—determined by the leaves that grant shadow to the hawk eating his food" (ibid.). According to Testart et al. (2004), comparison is the main feature of measurement, and the difference between counting and measuring is stressed. While counting relies on numbers of already visible pieces, or those divided for the occasion, measurement requires similarity or comparison since "there is no measurement without a standard" (ibid.: 10). The relation of leaves to the hawk's body forms such a model unit, and the rural law decree thus complies with a minimum definition of ethno-metrology.

In these cases, quantification, measuring, and the formation of units do not shape the material to give exact amounts; instead, they create comparisons of existent sizes and forms. There are four characteristics of the measurement practices that Grimm collects, quotes, and documents from juridical sources: (1) they are all non-numerical; (2) they are situated in rural settings; (3) they decide possession or usufruct, just as a purchase with money; and (4) they are presented vividly, rendering dynamic the relations of persons and amounts. Through such presentation, the physical relations of bodies gain a functional form. In an early article, Grimm (1815b) describes such intimacy between things, animals, and persons, as 'poetic'.[2] It is not only the multiplicity of qualities that makes these measurements noteworthy for investigations of money's quantitative and material aspects. Grimm also sees a liberal tendency in these 'poetic' elements of law: "Finally I have to count as a proof of the poetry that [resides] in the old law the lightheartedness of the latter: by this I understand the tendency not to pin down each and every thing and to prescribe fixed measurements for people" (ibid.: 189).

Qualities, relations, and sizes serve as approximate measures. They give no fixed amounts that could serve as prescriptions for action, but leave things open, requiring negotiation. Measurements are incomplete without further decisions by local actors. One rural decree on water regulation shows this openness when stipulating the level to which a millstream could be dammed. This example, which was frequently quoted by Grimm, originated in a fertile region north of Frankfurt on the Main, the Wetterau: "The water shall be adjusted to a level and the miller shall not raise his weir above [a point] that a bee [landing] on a nail's head that is right in the middle of the pole [is able to] support itself and drink and enjoy the water [with its] feet and wings unharmed and unmoistened" (cited in Stengel 1886: 109). Evoking the natural milieu of a small insect, this decree creates precision through imagery. A shifting, precarious zone between the bee's leg and the waterline indicates a narrow range of tolerance for the miller wishing to augment his main energy source. The mode of description may be easily memorized, but offers neither decisive amounts nor measures. The pole's length and the nail's location remain subject to negotiations beyond the law.

Grimm (1815b) characterizes these procedural measurements as 'poetic' in a way that he discerns from poetical language. Contrary to preconceived notions, this 'poetic' kind of object relation resides in measurement: "Poetic regulations are found first and foremost in the imaginations of space and time when it has to be determined how far something is supposed to reach and how long it is supposed to last" (ibid.: 169). Such regulations entrust bodies, actions, and things to determine sizes, borders, and effective dates. According to Grimm ([1828] 1992: 103), ancient rules shun numbers in favor of simple procedures. For example, conventionally known measures such as 'ell' or 'foot' are mentioned in the 'poetic' descriptions, but the issue to be determined by them is never fully determined. The model unit consists of an image that serves as a frame for further agreement. The main issue—for example, millstream water levels—is under-determined, while minor elements—the bee's situation—are highly detailed. Grimm (1815b: 174) suggests that the dysfunctionality of such measures, in this case, their vagueness, is their virtue: "Above all the old German law prefers a lighthearted approach when it comes to bestowals and easements, which grants more room to the free play of rough estimation than to dry words. The dues, which are described in detail in the most sensual and detailed way, remain ambiguous when it comes to the main contract." Their ambiguity makes these measurements valuable for Grimm because key issues are left for local actors to decide in the regions where these law codes apply. Thus, the crucial addendum to qualitative or 'poetic' quantification is an element of decision making or judgment. But it would be a severe misjudgment of Jacob Grimm's broader aims to understand these procedures as a fair, egalitarian, and enlightened type of rationality alone. Negotiation is situated between aggressive confrontation and deliberations among equals, between established claims and granted fairness, and between personal interest and justice.

Although Grimm was fervently democratic in his ancient law studies and a defender of the right to self-rule in the periphery,[3] there was hardly a more committed, outspoken enemy of French egalitarianism and civic codes, let alone the political hopes that went with the introduction of the metric system during the French Revolution. Thus, Grimm's theory of measurement is part of a larger argument. For the current question of qualitative measurement, this political and juridical context is important insofar as it prompts Grimm to invent a complex, innovative concept of quantification. His space of negotiation is not a place where equals meet and come to terms; instead, it is open to hierarchical and asymmetric relations. Qualitative quantification cannot be subsumed as 'pre-modern' and 'embedded' or as 'modern' and 'disembedded' from the social sphere because this space involves the (aggressive) negotiations of free actors. Procedural measurements are predecessors of numerical quantification and include elements that are today no longer linked to measurement.

There are three characteristics of procedural measurements to mention. Along with his chapter on measures, Grimm describes the role of symbols, numbers, and chance. These are prominent parts in all elements of ancient law, and they significantly distinguish procedural measurements from scientific ones. When performed in public space, measurements themselves gain a symbolic dimension. Procedural measurements must be understood as performative (Fischer-Lichte 2004) when conducted in public space, for example, when bowshots fired in a circular direction determine where to build the moat around a city. Perception of the environment is irrevocably altered by these symbolic measurements. Grimm deems this a kind of 'sacralization of borders'. Such a performance is advantageous in comparison with mere measuring: "A secular measure would have been much easier, [but] would not have sacralized the cessions and acquisitions" (Grimm 1815b: 173). Public measuring performances thus lend authority to the result. Grimm even compares such actions with notarization (ibid.: 179). This indicates a functional necessity to perform measures instead of simply stating them verbally or in written form.

Taking up the bee example again, the actual decree is very specific about all the conditions that must accompany the adjustment of water levels. It uses symbols and is itself a symbolic action. The *Wetterauer Wassergerichtsweisthum* lists many stipulations that lend lasting authority to the nail on which the bee is saved. The nail is to be adorned with flowers and colorful lace; it is to be carried by a boy to the river, followed by a beautifully dressed girl. The water judges and a water captain give it three strikes with a hammer after they have dispensed with parts of their festive attire, and they must sing during the procedure. Afterward, they are required to distribute fruits or red linen to the public. Their names and dates of baptism are written on a piece of waxed paper that is affixed to the pole as well. Writing techniques of notarization were used, although they appear slightly out of place. In the same way, measuring technology was involved. Grimm does not mention this in *Deutsche Rechtsalterthümer*, but a version of the directive he publishes in his *Weisthümer* clearly states that the tradition includes a "little silver balance."[4] It is carried to the stream in a procession by the judges, who—in Grimm's account—are in control of the procedure and decide the nail's position, while the measuring instrument plays a minor part.

Grimm's contemporaries and later scholars voiced doubts about this assumption of symbolic actions. They questioned the particular language of the rural law decrees, or Weistümer, arguing that these measurements were theatrical rather than performative. From this perspective, these astonishing passages are not symbolic acts being performed but merely ornamental descriptions read to a village assembly. The listeners' expectations become a key driving force for presenting improbable, remarkable practices invented for public entertainment (Hertel 2005: 48; Hübner 1895: 122). Generally, Grimm writes polemically, and tends to include what supports his aims, but in the case of the *Wetterauer Wassergerichtsweisthum*, festive procedures do comply with the findings on customary law. Contracts took forms that were much closer to actions. Since the discovery of all kinds of customary, non-codified law, performative and symbolic dimensions have been recognized as essential features (Girard [1918] 2003; Michelet [1837] 2009). The famous jurist, Friedrich Carl von Savigny (1814: 10), even identifies formalized actions (*förmliche Handlungen*) as the "grammar of law."

Grimm's account of numbers, when they accompany procedural measurements, also involves actions. His quotations and examples point toward practices that equate referential numbers and measuring practices. Numbers do not indicate abstracting processes but rather signal well-established routines of sharing, scheduling, and distribution. In Grimm's ([1828] 1992: 285) sources, uneven numbers, such as three, seven, and nine, play a key role in organizing social institutions. These customary numbers determine the distribution of land, payments, time-scales, and other "things, periods, and actions" (ibid.). Grimm's examples, assembled during a period when communal possession of grazing land was widely discussed, very often express the traditional usufruct rights that he advocated. Accordingly, an examination of common use rights, or slackening of property rules, appears in a section about the number three. The rule 'three are free' allowed travelers to acquire three turnips or pieces of fruit found alongside roads. Grimm emphasizes guest rights as a vital aspect of the common law of the people. Likewise, wagoners were free to feed three sheaves to their oxen in passing, but only if they did not carry away any grain or leave remains on the ground (ibid.: 287). Such use of numbers points to a script for old customs instead of abstract amounts, to concrete quantification instead of numbering.

Chance is the third and last element that distinguishes procedural measurements from scientific notions. During procedures that decide land ownership and other property rights, there are not only ambiguities but also processes that cannot be entirely controlled, such as throwing objects. The opening chapter of *Deutsche Rechtsalterthümer* lists 60 instances of objects that can be thrown. For example, hammers must be wielded right-handed, but under the left leg. Sometimes additional positions are involved, such as tossing backwards or holding onto a fence or animal during the action. These complications introduce chance in otherwise obvious measures of strength and skill (Grimm [1828] 1992: 92).

Another example of chance elements in procedural measurements comes from testament law. A directive on inheritance requires 'appeasing' older laws of primogeniture. The eldest son inherits marginally more land than his brothers, although in principle they share the estate equally. The eldest son's surplus is not a fixed surface measure: it is left to the "arbitrariness of an innocent animal" (Grimm 1815b: 171). A rooster's flight designates the super-additum: "He receives in addition to his share the flight of a rooster's amount of land, as much as a flying rooster, left to glide, crosses before it lands" (ibid.). Even a strong, motivated animal will not designate more than a symbolic piece of land. Such procedures delegate part of the decision to an open interplay of personal and material forces. Procedural measurements provocatively include the influence of the surroundings.

Few things stand so overtly in contrast to the idea of a just, transparent, and controllable measurement than this involuntary formation of the units in question, especially in a juridical context. By incorporating circumstantial influence, procedural measurements lose claims to justice and contradict ideas of fairness. The space within which Grimm's measurements operate is not the fixed, reliable matrix that the metric system presupposes. Yet in this cooperation of uncontrollable bodies and local processes, decisions are not absent, and rational agreement is reached while accepting external circumstances. A surprising account of quantification that is neither balanced nor able to build fair equivalents emerges. Grimm (1815b: 170) argues that private law or measurement in economic or fiscal situations is frequently part of asymmetric relations: "The new law wants to be exhaustive and anticipate all cases, [while] the old one dreads at times to intervene and delegates the decision to something natural, accidental. It honors holy numbers, while [the new law] tends to prescribe dead and secular numbers and tends to measure with them." While one law feigns comprehensive control of all cases and 'prescribes' numbers, the other type is described in rather unconventional terms as being prone to delegation and hesitant to interfere. Qualitative quantifications—or, as Grimm suggests, 'poetic' measures—have one thing in common: they are scripts that set existing, natural entities into relation with each other. The final formation of units always depends on a mixture of rational discourse, symbolic actions, and circumstances, if not fate.

This makes the question of what Grimm has to say about money all the more interesting. Money has been compared to a measure from Aristotle onward (cf. Seitz, this volume) despite the fact that measures of physical dimensions differ remarkably from any measure of value. Measurement relies on natural phenomena that can be determined by empirical proof, while value is a much more elusive measure of intensity and depends on individual personal perceptions. As discussed in the next part of this chapter, Grimm touches on the question of monetary value several times, chiefly in the form of monetary payment for injury.

## Procedural Measurement of Value: Injured Bodies and Money's Origin

In *Deutsche Rechtsalterthümer*, Grimm ([1828] 1992) classifies procedural measurements according to sensual experiences and physical actions, such as touch, sound, throwing, walking around fields, and sitting. His subchapter on sound is rather close in content to subsequent passages titled "Man's Strength" and "Measurement of Wounds." In all of these, Grimm quotes passages on the determination of possessions or on the right to rule. In effect, dominion extends as far away as instruments or animal voices can be heard. But sound may be put to use as a more complex measure: it may test monetary value. Grimm gives an example of tax payment procedures from early modern Frisia (cf. Emmius [1596–1616] 1981; Grimm 1815b: 108). The payment took place in a house with 12 chambers. In the first, a representative of the authority waited. In the last was an iron shield known as a *Klippschild* (Grimm [1828] 1992: 103), whose name evokes the clicking sound of things thrown onto it. Frisian taxpayers were required to drop coins into this metallic vessel. Their contributions were valid only if the noise of falling coins was audible to the official listening 12 chambers away. The procedure is peculiar because the amount owed was not prescribed by number or by the name of the coin, although payment was in coins, not in kind. Neither denominational values nor payment by sight counted (ibid.: 108).

Grimm does not discuss whether this procedure, described in a legendary historical account, might have proved more precise and reliable because many institutions issued and forged currencies (cf. Conway 2012). The history of numismatics is rich in examples of this kind of testing by ear (Steed 2015). But Grimm's ([1828] 1992) conclusions point in another direction. According to him, this procedure attempted to settle how much citizens owed. The element of personal freedom of choice is palpable in this particular passage. The *Klippschild* guaranteed only that a certain minimum value would be transferred. Since this could be verified by ear, the sound would allow for just the right amount of knowledge and discretion. As in the qualitative measurement of material, the qualitative measurement of value comprises not just complex judgments of material amounts, but also reflections on what is due.

Grimm ([1828] 1992: 110) supports the measurement of value by sound with further examples that he describes as unusual and surprising. No less than 11 quotes that describe measuring injuries with sounds are provided from medieval German law codices. Noise is made by throwing bones into a metal vessel: splinters incapable of producing sounds indicate negligible injuries unworthy of compensation. Thus, acoustic volume measures the graveness of the injury and answers the question of what must be paid.

Contrary to the example above, where the sound of money in a vessel might have been a reliable indicator of a coin's poor ore content, or might have helped determine the metal percentage of foreign, unknown denominations, the measurement of bones seems to have little practical advantage. But, unlikely as it seems, quantification of injuries is established beyond doubt in major law codes of the Early Middle Ages. In contrast to the many improbable measuring practices that Grimm discusses, tariffs for different injuries form a substantial part of the medieval wergild system. The western *Leges Alamannorum* discern lesions of the upper and under eyelid, while the northern *Lex Frisionum* names the joints of every finger. Most of these law codes, dating from the sixth to the ninth century, state that the killing of a free person must be compensated with wergild of 200 solidi (gold coins). Payment was transferred from family to family, establishing a system of checks and balances that is usually looked on as a means to prevent revenge and feuds (Wallace-Hadrill 1959). Amounts differed regionally and were augmented or diminished according to the social status of the parties involved. Servants had no wergild, only a price. Derived from this payment were the diverse tariffs for all kinds of injuries, thus quantifying injury and pain. In this context, Lisi Oliver (2011: 72–111) does not find the strange weighting of bones by sound unlikely. Combining medical history and archaeological evidence of healed skulls, she argues that there is reason to measure even pieces of skulls in the ancient cases quoted by Grimm, since people could survive the injury.

Such critical reasoning based on sources was not Grimm's approach. He never aimed to be a historian in the historicist sense of the word; instead, he was concerned with traces and forgotten remnants of ancient times. The 3,000 rural law decrees that he collected and edited are a monument to this aim of simultaneously preserving and inventing a German tradition (Grimm [1840–1878] 2000: vi; Werkmüller 1972). Medievalist Ulrich Wyss (1979: 289) therefore distinguishes Jacob Grimm's collecting from that of his brother Wilhelm and other newly professionalized text philologists of the day, calling it a type of "wild philology."

Ironically, the ensemble of the Germanic *leges barbarorum*, the so-called laws of the barbarians, from various countries is perceived in a very similar light today. The proximity of these rules to Roman law is often stressed, but it is also understood that lawmaking in the Early Middle Ages tried to establish distance from all things Roman. Patrick Wormald (2003: 32) argues that emerging states used the new codifications as a tool for what he calls "ethnic engineering." Thus, the tariff lists do not mirror existing, let alone Germanic, customs; instead, they prescribe a region in which this seemingly archaic wergild vocabulary was offered for identification and nation building. At the same time, wergild appears as an almost standardized system throughout Europe, while currencies or weights and measures—as visible marks of a state's presence—were fragmented into numerous systems.

The wergild system is noteworthy when discussing the materiality of money's quantity because it has been identified as a crucial step in the historical development of money. Although Paul Einzig (1948) mentions an array of potential origin stories—state taxation, markets, hoarding, ornaments—he points in the direction of wergild as the most likely candidate. Even in chartalist theories (Wray 2004: 79–98), where money is considered to be a creature of the controlling state, wergild has long been considered an important precondition. The numismatist Philip Grierson (1978: 11) concludes that the first necessary function of money that had to be developed would have been a valid, widely accepted standard: "Money as a standard in fact lies behind money as a medium of exchange." Therefore, metrology and quantifying practices are central to the development of money and historically precede the exchange function. Grierson explicitly refers to the problem of measuring value (ibid.):

> Our task is not essentially different from that of the student of other systems of measurement, though it is a much more complex one ... Units of value, like units of area, volume, and weight, could only be arrived at with great difficulty, in part because natural units are absent, in part because of the much greater diversity of commodities that had to be measured and the consequent difficulty of finding common standards in terms of which they could reasonably be compared.

First, a scale had to be established against which reliable intersubjective equivalents could be measured. Grierson (1978: 13) designates a juridical scene as the most likely context for the first development of money, with reference to Anglo-Saxon wergild catalogues:

> The conditions under which these laws were put together would appear to satisfy, much better than any market mechanism, the prerequisites for the establishment of a monetary system. The tariffs for damages were established in public assemblies, and the common standards were based on objects of some value which a householder might be expected to possess or which he could obtain from his kinsfolk. Since what is laid down consists of evaluations of injuries, not evaluations of commodities, the conceptual difficulty of devising a common measure for appraising unrelated objects is avoided.

Before returning to the problem of how Grimm aligned the fixed tariffs with his ideas on ambiguous procedural measurement, the existence of a currency in the wergild system has to be addressed. Grierson's argument is deployed against the theory that money originated in peaceful market exchanges in fair cooperation. But most ancient law codes clearly designate amounts in a monetary currency—solidus, the Roman (and later Byzantine) unit of gold—and coins circulated long before the first wergild catalogue is reported. Monetary units seem to accompany wergild tariffs.

Nevertheless, there is much support for the thesis that money has something to do with the principle of 'violent exchange', precisely because the payment of blood money is not an absolute exchange. It remains incomplete and can therefore be seen as a transient practice. In a wergild payment, one side receives money, but the other side does not obtain a product. The compensation sets the murderer free from persecution, if not guilt. Karl Polanyi (1977: 106) draws a connection between payment and a special approach toward moral states of shame: "Punishment approximates payment when the process of riddance of guilt is quantified." For David Graeber (2011: 171), Irish wergild catalogues are but one example of the important role that social values played in determining "measures of honor and degradation: that is, the value of money was, ultimately, the value of the power to turn others into money." Graeber stresses that the violence was twofold: displacing persons from their previous settings and relations, and gaining power over them by monetary means. Thus, Grimm's high interest in the measurement of wounds is in keeping with monetary pre-history and anthropological findings. Loss of body parts or life was a palpable, visible quantification of value. Such measures segmented intensity into units. Violence toward bodies thus created a widely recognized measure of value. Grimm knew the social hierarchies and tariffs of all *leges barbarorum* very accurately, as his calculations on the value of a life in each respective law code illustrate (see fig. 1).

Grimm does not develop the wergild system into a monetary or abstract payment, but rather into concrete practices, which is where the parallels with procedural measurements begin. In doing so, Grimm reverses the perspective. While wergild is considered a precursor of money, Grimm searches for the precursor of wergild tariffs. His account of the system hinges on the problem of building equivalents between human beings and material value and provides a pre-monetary solution. Grimm (1815a: 145) presents measures for injury or death as ways to reach an agreement that does not restore justice, since, in his opinion, "one cannot measure the worth of two lives against one another." Revenge or payment are two possible options, but neither offers equivalence, so he introduces wergild as a remedy—not to replace the loss, but to 'appease' the relatives, deterring them from further action. This is why wergild is not subsumed under punishments but under penitence in his *Deutsche Rechtsalter-thümer*. Once again, Grimm focuses on measuring procedures: "One believed in finding the highest reparation for the life of the deceased in the most noble metal, gold; furthermore, [one thought] to come closest to it through a bodily weighting and counterweighting" (ibid.: 147).

Grimm's main concern is deriving the wergild system from the physical act of determining a body's weight in gold or covering it with gold. His main reference is undoubtedly the *Edda*, a collection of poems about Old Norse legends. When Loki proudly presents the skin of a slain otter to his host in gratitude, the man recognizes one of his sons, who had been a shapeshifter, and instantly demands wergild. But he does not demand the typical 200 solidi or another fixed, quantified amount. Instead, the skin is filled and outwardly covered, not in money, but in gold. The exact expression—'to cover and to fill', or *hüllen und füllen*—still forms a well-known German alliteration indi-cating abundant amounts, with enough to spare (Anon. 1896). Instead of weighing a person against gold, Grimm suggests that the physical coverage and remodeling of the body are the procedures at the center of the inven-tion of wergild. However, neither a body's weight in gold nor covering a body in it are directly linked to wergild payments in existing historical law codices. Grimm finds adjacent rules in the comprehensive code of the Sax-ons, the *Sachsenspiegel*, where a killed dog is covered in wheat, a practice also reported from the Netherlands and even some Arabic countries (Grimm 1815a: 149). But, all in all, Grimm seems to embark on a quest against his sources. The history of law shows only very weak traces of concrete equiva-lences built from dead bodies themselves and valuable matter that was to cover them completely. Although ceremonies involving the weighing of bodies in

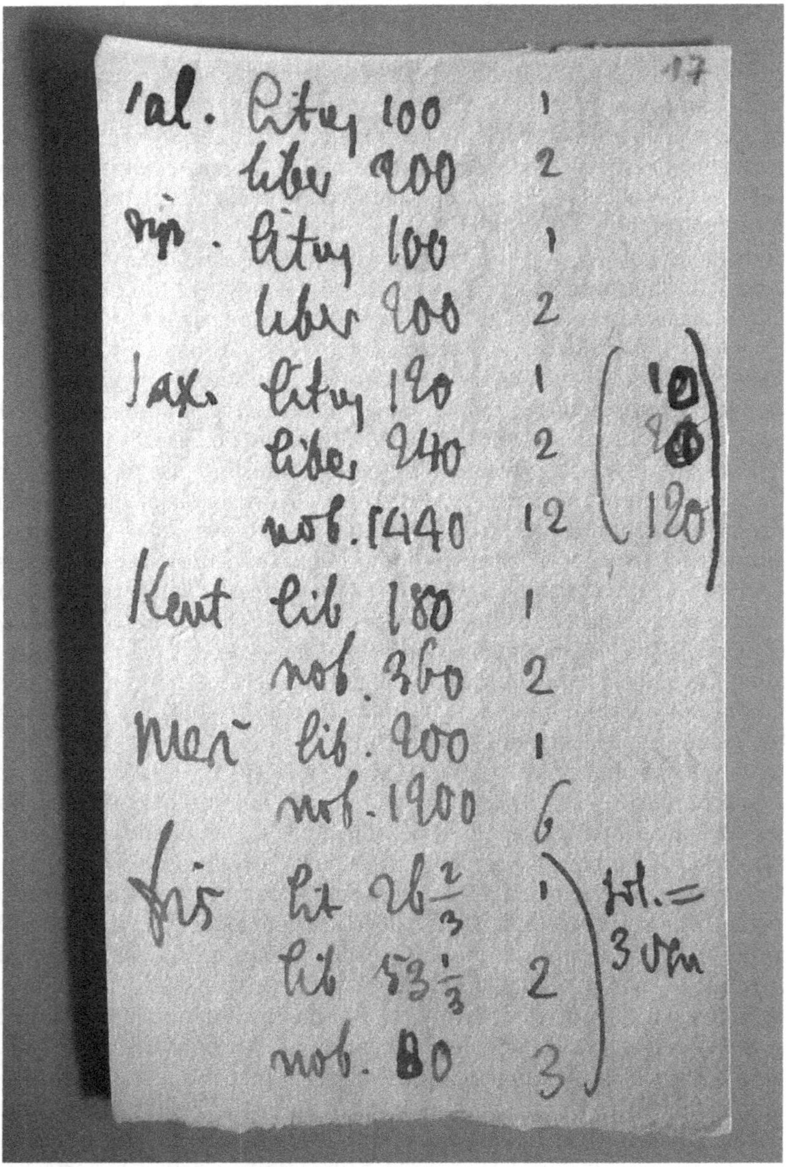

sal. litus 100    1
     liber 200    2
rip. litus 100    1
     liber 200    2
sax. litus 120    1    ( 10
     liber 240    2      20
     nob. 1440   12    ( 120 )
Kent lib 180      1
     nob. 360     2
Mer lib. 200      1
     nob. 1900    6
fris lit 26⅔      1   ) sol. =
     lib 53⅓      2   ) 3 sm.
     nob. 80      3

**FIGURE 1:** Jacob Grimm determines the value of a person using wergild tariffs according to Lex Salica, Lex Ripuaria, Lex Saxonum, Lex Frisionum, and others. While a free person (liber) calls for twice as much wergild compared to a lower-class person (litus), the remuneration for killing a noble varies. Used with permission of Staatsbibliothek zu Berlin–Preußischer Kulturbesitz, Handschriftenabteilung NG 289, no. 17.

gold abound (Schaffer 2015), they are not part of the wergild system. One might wonder why Grimm insisted on the link.

Grimm's invented genealogy of the widely spread penal law system inverts the relationship of body and number. In the famous lists of tariffs, every limb, hand, or head has a price and a fixed number attached to it that designates the worth of redemption payments. What Grimm constructs as the beginning of the practice is a one-to-one relation of shapes, where the dead body—or its fur and skin—performs as a measure of value. No numbers are involved, but the physical characteristics of size, and sometimes weight, determine compensation. Again, Grimm is not concerned with the process of abstraction. He deploys all his skills as a philologist, etymologist, and historian of law to evoke the opposite and read 'backward' into forms of concrete quantification. The "Measurement of Wounds" gives a tautological answer to the question of how qualitative quantification arrives at a measure of value: the victim's body is turned into a genuine measure for itself. The dead body designates the almost arbitrary amount of gold or grain that should be handed down to the family of the deceased. Accounts are not balanced, but are nevertheless kept.

## Conclusion

The documented practices that Grimm discusses in rural law codes are ambiguous, imprecise, and 'poetic'. Yet they seem functional for organizing the materiality of exchange and settling disputes over possessions. It is crucial that no fixed amounts are given, since qualitative quantification is able to open up space for negotiation. If numbers occur, they are used more like symbols or scripts for performative actions. Contrary to the very idea of the standardized, internationalized metric system of the nineteenth century, Grimm argues for the inclusion of chance elements, thus abandoning claims to justice and a transparent, reliable matrix for measurement.

Grimm's focus on procedural measurements shows that the sizes and shapes of objects suffice as points of reference. Concerning the special case of quantification of value, he argues that even blood money is derived from a non-numerical process. It may not open a positive space for negotiation, but it is clearly discussed as a tool to settle disputes between complex networks of families and interests. Although the quantification of value is less benign than the procedures to measure materials, both are used to come to terms, despite a good deal of resultant injustice. These astonishing findings for an analysis of legal codes render a picture of quantification and measurement that is grounded in a certain futility. Equivalents can be built by using a rooster to designate an arbitrary piece of land to be inherited, but it remains impossible to translate the value of a once living being—be it man or dog.

In both analyzed cases—the quantification of physical space and of value—Grimm sees the same logic at work. His concrete quantifications do not provide 'just' or 'fair' amounts based on natural facts; they resolve conflicts only to a degree, within an uncontrolled, and uncontrollable, space of accepted asymmetric relations. They operate on a different level of precision, where ambiguity makes a social encounter and its subsequent settling of conflict necessary. Grimm's account of quantification thus dispenses with the qualitative-quantitative dichotomy. He deviates at the very point where the 'poetic' measures are coupled with the free discretion of individual actors. The ancient qualitative society is thus not binding, nor is it in any way 'warmer', more 'relational', or 'social'. On the contrary, the wergild system perpetuates a stratified society: the space of negotiation is framed as an arena wherein the forceful win the day and relations are profoundly asymmetrical. This discharge of just procedures is amplified by chance, which establishes a topological space that is far less controllable than the space modern measurements take for granted.

Grimm deplores the pretensions of the newly introduced metric system, propagated in the same legal documents as modernized jurisprudence. The precise measurements of modernity held no egalitarian promise, but instead posed the threat of centralized prescription and command. At the same time, these measures externalize judgment to binding numbers, which leaves Grimm's portrait of cherished strategies of the French Enlightenment—of all things—devoid of rationality. Thus, abstraction and quantification are not neutral, but downright dictatorial and oblivious of negotiation, while 'poetic' measurement, as presented by Grimm, emerges at times as a democratic and comparatively reasonable form of measurement.

## Acknowledgments

Work on this chapter was funded by the Max Planck Institute for the History of Science. I wish to thank Lukas Bothe, Lorraine Daston, Minakshi Menon, Christine von Oertzen, and Andreas Wolfsteiner for their invaluable comments. I am grateful to Shawn Kendrick, Mario Schmidt, and Sandy Ross for their advice and guidance, which helped shape this chapter.

---

**Anna Echterhölter** is a Professor of the History of Science at the University of Vienna. She has been a Research Assistant at Humboldt University and has held fellowships at the Max Planck Institute for the History of Science in Berlin and the German Historical Institute in Washington, DC. She is currently investigating the economy of weights and measures and the political metallurgy of copper. A founding member of the research journal *ilinx*, she is a co-author, with Hendrik Blumentrath, Frederike Felcht, and Karin Harrasser, of *Jenseits des Geldes: Aporien der Rationierung* (2019).

## Notes

1. Unless otherwise indicated, all text translations are my own.
2. Such 'poetic' forms of qualitative quantification are under-explored in most analyses of commerce and taxation, although they have been described elsewhere. See, for example, Gudeman (1986: 10) on labor-seed relations, Hocquet et al. (1989: 90) on units of force, such as a wagonload or *charretée*, and Menon (2013: 10–14) on British Raj taxation.
3. Necessary criticisms of Grimm's account of ancient German law should be mentioned. Much could also be said about the direct political reverberations of his account of measurements within his own time as well. The role of judges in the ancient documents mirrors claims of the Historical School of Law with which Grimm was strongly affiliated. The faction of the 'Germanists' especially turned ancient Germanic law into a political argument for more democratic rights (Dilcher and Kern 1984). The very genre of law decree or Weistum was read as a proof of self-rule of the people—an interpretation that has been considerably contested and differentiated by historians of law (Algazi 1997; Stolleis 2001; Teuscher 2007). Although once believed to be progressive, many motives of this juridical movement received a fatal reception during the Third Reich.
4. It is possible that the balance is a water level. The directive uses the phrase 'small silver balance' (*kleine silberne Wage*) twice. But a few lines earlier, Grimm describes the millers as people who are "derer Wasser und derselben Wagen und Kunst erfahren" (experienced in the art of measuring with scales and water levels). The 'vindication', 'probation', and 'justification' of the pole seem to guarantee its upright position. However, references to the precious metal and the small size of the balance hint at a symbolic use. In the end, the decisive element is the nail in the pole, and there is no mention of how its height could be determined with a balance (Anon. [1611] 2000: 464).

## References

Alder, Ken. 1998. "Making Things the Same: Representation, Tolerance and the End of the *Ancien Régime* in France." *Social Studies of Science* 28 (4): 499–545.

Algazi, Gadi. 1997. "Lords Ask, Peasants Answer: Making Traditions in Late-Medieval Village Assemblies." In *Between History and Histories: The Making of Silences and Commemorations*, ed. Gerald Sider and Gavin Smith, 199–229. Toronto: University of Toronto Press.

Anonymous. (1611) 2000. *Wetterauer Wassergerichtsweisthum*. In *Jacob und Wilhelm Grimm: Werke*, ed. Ludwig Erich Schmitt and Dieter Werkmüller. Abteilung I, vol. 21, part 3, 463–470. Hildesheim: Olms.

Anonymous. 1896. "Article: Hülle." In *Deutsches Wörterbuch von Jacob und Wilhelm Grimm*, vol. 10. Leipzig: Hirzel.

Conway, Joe. 2012. "Making Beautiful Money: Currency Connoisseurship in the Nineteenth-Century United States." *Nineteenth-Century Contexts: An Interdisciplinary Journal* 34 (5): 427–443.

Dalton, George. 1965. "Primitive Money." *American Anthropologist* 67 (1): 44–65.

Dilcher, Gerhard, and Rüdiger Kern. 1984. "Die juristische Germanistik des 19. Jahrhunderts und die Fachtradition der Deutschen Rechtsgeschichte." *Zeitschrift der Savigny-Stiftung für Rechtsgeschichte, Germanistische Abteilung* 101: 1–46.

Dodd, Neigel. 2005. "Laundering 'Money': On the Need for Conceptual Clarity within the Sociology of Money." *Archives européennes de sociologie* 46 (3): 387–411.

Dommann, Monika, Christoph Dejung, and Daniel Speich Chassé, eds. 2014. *Auf der Suche nach der Ökonomie: Historische Annäherungen.* Tübingen: Mohr Siebeck.

Einzig, Paul. 1948. "New Light on the Origin of Money." *Nature* 162 (4130): 983–985.

Emmius, Ubbo. (1596–1616) 1981. *Friesische Geschichte (Rerum Frisicarum historiae libri 60).* 6 vols. Trans. Erich von Reeken. Frankfurt: Wörner.

Engster, Frank. 2014. *Das Geld als Maß, Mittel und Methode: Das Rechnen mit der Identität der Zeit.* Berlin: Neofelis.

Fischer-Lichte, Erika. 2004. *Ästhetik des Performativen.* Frankfurt: Suhrkamp.

Frängsmyr, Tore, J. L. Heilbron, and Robin E. Rider, eds. 1990. *The Quantifying Spirit in the Eighteenth Century.* Berkeley: University of California Press.

Girard, Paul. (1918) 2003. *Manuel élémentaire de droit romain.* Paris: Dalloz.

Gooday, Graeme. 2004. *The Morals of Measurement: Accuracy, Irony, and Trust in Late Victorian Electrical Practice.* Cambridge: Cambridge University Press.

Graeber, David. 2011. *Debt: The First 5,000 Years.* Brooklyn, NY: Melville House.

Grierson, Philip. 1978. "The Origins of Money." *Research in Economic Anthropology* 1 (1): 1–35.

Grimm, Jacob. (1815a) 1991. "Über eine eigene altgermanische weise der mordsühne." In *Jacob und Wilhelm Grimm: Werke,* ed. Ludwig Erich Schmitt, Abteilung I, vol. 6, Rezensionen und vermischte Aufsätze 1, 144–152. Hildesheim: Olms.

Grimm, Jacob. (1815b) 1991. "Von der poesie im recht." In *Jacob und Wilhelm Grimm: Werke,* ed. Ludwig Erich Schmitt, Abteilung I, vol. 6, Rezensionen und vermischte Aufsätze 1, 152–191. Hildesheim: Olms.

Grimm, Jacob. (1828) 1992. *Deutsche Rechtsalterthümer.* In *Jacob und Wilhelm Grimm: Werke,* ed. Ludwig Erich Schmitt, Abteilung I, vols. 17 and 18. Hildesheim: Olms. Reprint of the 4th ed. dated 1899.

Grimm, Jacob. (1840–1878) 2000. *Weisthümer.* In *Jacob und Wilhelm Grimm: Werke,* Abteilung I, vols. 19–25. From the edition of Jacob Grimm, Erich Dronke, and Heinrich Beyer, ed. and with an introduction by Dieter Werkmüller. Hildesheim: Olms.

Gudeman, Stephen. 1986. *Economics as Culture: Models and Metaphors of Livelihood.* London: Routledge.

Guyer, Jane I. 2004. *Marginal Gains: Monetary Transactions in Atlantic Africa.* Chicago: Chicago University Press.

Guyer, Jane I. 2011. "Soft Currencies, Cash Economies, New Monies: Past and Present." *Proceedings of the National Academy of Sciences* 109 (7): 2214–2221.

Hertel, Volker. 2005. "Thüringische Dorfordnungen und Weistümer im Gefüge ländlicher Kommunikation." In *Die ländliche Gemeinde im Spätmittelalter: Deidesheimer Gespräche zur Sprach- und Kulturgeschichte,* ed. Albrecht Greule and Jörg Meier, 37–58. Berlin: Weidler.

Hocquet, Jean-Claude, Bernhard Garnier, and Denis Woronoff, eds. 1989. *Introduction à la métrologie historique.* Paris: Economica.

Hübner, Rudolf. 1895. *Jacob Grimm und das deutsche Recht.* Göttingen: Dieterich.

Kula, Witold. 1986. *Measures and Men.* Trans. Richard Szreter. Princeton, NJ: Princeton University Press.

Maye, Harun. 2010. "Was ist eine Kulturtechnik?" *Zeitschrift für Medien- und Kulturforschung* 1 (1): 121–135.

Menon, Minakshi. 2013. "Making Useful Knowledge: British Naturalists in Colonial India, 1784–1820." PhD diss., University of California.

Michelet, Jules. (1837) 2009. *Origines du droit français cherchées dans les symboles et formules du droit universel.* Cergy: Pagala.

Oliver, Lisi. 2011. *The Body Legal in Barbarian Law*. Toronto: University of Toronto Press.

Polanyi, Karl. 1977. "Money Objects and Money Uses." In *The Livelihood of Man*, ed. Harry W. Pearson, 97–121. London: Academic Press.

Porter, Theodore M. 1995. *Trust in Numbers: The Pursuit of Objectivity in Science and Public Life*. Princeton, NJ: Princeton University Press.

Renner, Kaspar. 2012. "Archäologie des Rechts: Zur Geschichte einer vergessenen Disziplin zwischen Jacob Grimm, Karl von Amira und Michel Foucault." In *Literatur der Archäologie: Materialität und Rhetorik im 18. und 19. Jahrhundert*, ed. Jörn Lang and Jan Broch, 75–105. Munich: Fink.

Ross, Sandy. 2013. "What Is Ambiguous about Ambiguous Goods?" *Journal of Consumer Behaviour* 13 (2): 140–147.

Savigny, Friedrich Carl von. 1814. *Vom Beruf unserer Zeit für Gesetzgebung und Rechtswissenschaft*. Heidelberg: Mohr & Zimmer.

Schaffer, Simon. 1997. "Metrology, Metrication, and Victorian Values." *Victorian Science in Context*, ed. Bernard Lightman, 438–474. Chicago: University of Chicago Press.

Schaffer, Simon. 2000. "Modernity and Metrology." In *Science and Power: The Historical Foundations of Research Policies in Europe*, ed. Luca Guzzetti, 71–91. Luxembourg: Office for Official Publications of the European Communities.

Schaffer, Simon. 2015. "Les cérémonies de la mesure: Repenser l'histoire mondiale des sciences." *Annales: Histoire, Sciences Sociales* 70 (2): 409–435.

Schabacher, Gabriele. 2013. "Medium Infrastruktur: Trajektorien soziotechnischer Netzwerke in der ANT." *Zeitschrift für Medien- und Kulturforschung* 2: 129–148.

Schlaudt, Oliver. 2009. *Messung als konkrete Handlung: Eine kritische Untersuchung über die Grundlagen der Bildung quantitativer Begriffe in den Naturwissenschaften*. Heidelberg: Königshausen & Neumann.

Schmidt-Wiegand, Ruth, ed. 1999. *"Wörter und Sachen" als methodisches Prinzip und Forschungsrichtung*. 2 vols. Hildesheim: Olms.

Schoof, Wilhelm, ed. 1953. *Briefe der Brüder Grimm an Savigny*. Berlin: Schmidt.

Scott, James C. 1998. *Seeing Like a State: How Certain Schemes to Improve the Human Condition Have Failed*. New Haven, CT: Yale University Press.

Sibum, H. Otto. 1998. "Les gestes de la mesure: Joule, les pratiques de la brasserie et la science." *Annales: Histoire, Sciences Sociales* 53 (4–5): 745–774.

Steed, Emerson. 2015. "Coin Identification through Natural Frequency Analysis." Brigham Young University. https://me363.byu.edu/sites/me363.byu.edu/files/Emerson_Steed_CoinIdentification.pdf.

Stengel, Edmund, ed. 1886–1910. *Private und amtliche Beziehungen der Brüder Grimm zu Hessen: Eine Sammlung von Briefen und Actenstücken als Festschrift zum hundertsten Geburtstag Wilhelm Grimms den 24. Februar 1886*. 3 vols. Marburg: Elwert.

Stolleis, Michael. 2001. *Public Law in Germany 1800–1914*. New York: Berghahn Books.

Testart, Alain, Pierre Le Roux, Bernhard Sellato, and Jacques Ivanoff, eds. 2004. *Poids et mesures en Asie du Sud-Est: Systèmes métrologiques et sociétés*. Vol. 1. Paris: École française d'Extrême-Orient.

Teuscher, Simon. 2007. *Erzähltes Recht: Lokale Herrschaft, Verschriftlichung und Traditionsbildung im Spätmittelalter*. Frankfurt: Campus.

Verran, Helen. 2010. "Number as Inventive Frontier in Knowing and Working Australia's Water Resources." *Anthropological Theory* 10 (1–2): 171–178.

Wallace-Hadrill, John M. 1959. "The Bloodfeud of the Franks." *Bulletin of the John Rylands Library* 41: 459–487.

Wedell, Moritz. 2004. "Vom Kerbholz zum Kalkül: Wortgeschichtliche Annäherung an die Kulturtechnik Zahl." In *Grenzfälle: Transformationen von Bild, Schrift und Zahl,* ed. Pablo Schneider and Moritz Wedell, 65–100. Weimar: VDG.

Werkmüller, Dieter. 1972. *Über Aufkommen und Verbreitung der Weistümer: Nach der Sammlung von Jacob Grimm.* Berlin: Schmidt.

Wise, M. Norton, ed. 1995. *The Values of Precision.* Princeton, NJ: Princeton University Press.

Wormald, Patrick. 2003. "The *Leges Barbarorum*: Law and Ethnicity in the Post-Roman West." In *Regna and Gentes: The Relationship between Late Antique and Early Medieval Peoples and Kingdoms in the Transformation of the Roman World,* ed. Hans-Werner Goetz, Jörg Jarnut, and Walter Pohl, 21–54. Leiden: Brill.

Wray, L. Randall, ed. 2004. *Credit and State Theories of Money: The Contributions of A. Mitchell Innes.* Cheltenham: Edward Elgar.

Wyss, Ulrich. 1979. *Die wilde Philologie: Jacob Grimm und der Historismus.* Munich: Beck.

*Chapter 3*

# FIVE THOUSAND, 5,000, AND FIVE THOUSANDS
Disentangling Ruble Quantities and Qualities

*Sandy Ross*

If read aloud, the title of this chapter seems repetitive, but these terms indicate three analytical categories that distinguish the ways in which affluent migrants in urban Russia understand and manage money quantities at different levels of analysis. This chapter examines how people with particular norms about money usage adapt to environments with different expectations about money's quantities and material forms, using these accounts to question assumptions about money's 'natural' divisibility and to question (false) quantity-quality dichotomies. Rather than asserting that money's quantities are entangled with its qualities and materialities—per the currently fashionable dedifferentiation thesis (cf. Frankel 2015)—each category examines how quantities, qualities, and

Notes for this chapter begin on page 63.

materialities are bound up with one another in specific, contingent encounters. Affluent migrants' accounts highlight how quantities are used to create, or to imagine, relationships through money's quantitative nature, as denominations of great magnitude (Five Thousand); as sums beyond comfortable reckoning (5,000); and as calculable, precise, and/or accurate numbers (five thousands).

Writing about financial practices of low-income immigrants in Italy, Lazzer (2014) argues that migrants' accounts of money reveal mundane assumptions about money practices because they involve bridging gaps between money usage regimes. For example, affluent migrants in urban Russia expect that money quantities should be quantitatively and arithmetically divisible at any interval of the smallest currency unit: 1 ruble (or kopek), yen, cent, pence, and so on. A Fifty pound note buys a pint of milk for £1.12, with £48.88 change. Or, as my friend Miwako suggests, an *ichimanen* (10,000 yen) note is easily divided in corner shops for purchases as small as 50–100 yen. Yet Russian rubles are routinely not partible in this way. Some denominations are not divisible for purchases equal to, or below, their own order of magnitude. Taken-for-granted objects, such as money, present themselves most revealingly in moments of "unhandiness" (Heidegger [1927] 2010: 68). When expectations about what a thing should do or how it should behave are not met, we discover most clearly our own taken-for-granted assumptions. Each of the analytical terms in this chapter—Five Thousand, 5,000, and five thousands—identifies a set of moments when money presents itself as somehow 'unhandy'.

The first term, Five Thousand, reflects payment problems linked to indivisible magnitudes—usually One and Five Thousand denomination bank notes—and transactions where money resists being a technology of expenditure (Holbraad 2005). Five Thousand ruble notes are arithmetically divisible but are often refused because they are not practically partible. Moscow is predominantly a cash economy. Accustomed to electronic money, affluent migrants must relearn how to use cash: sorting notes and coins; the 'correct' note combinations; and informal, imprecise payment rules. Wallets and cashiers' tills become sites for collaborative payments where monies are reordered, evaluated, and (sometimes) explained. Using rubles well—in the (second) Aristotelian sense of excellence and skillful practice (Heidegger [1924] 2009: 55–56; cf. Seitz, this volume)—means knowing appropriate divisions, magnanimously accepting small losses or gains; and quickly producing desirable change. Using money well creates opportunities for claims about being part of, and set apart from, Russian urban society.

The second term, 5,000, indicates awkward sums, usually one to three orders larger than respondents had routinely handled. Upon their arrival in Russia, affluent migrants found Thousand and Five Thousand ruble bank notes shocking. These unfathomably large sums were interpreted as signs of disorder and disorganization in Russian society. Domesticating these 'big' sums involved vernacular social theorizing (Preda 2007) about perceived disorders/dysfunctions of Russian social and economic life. Dismayed reactions to, or critiques of, money offered coded ways to discuss disgust or frustration with Slavic Others (cf. Ross 2014). Qualities of money—bigness, unruliness, disorderliness—defined by quantitative attributes (the order of magnitude of monetary denominations) permitted moral boundary drawing (Lamont 1992) that contrasted 'Russian' cultural attributes and practices to 'rational', 'safe', non-Russian alternatives, producing fear and/or anxiety in the process.

The third term, five thousands, captures rubles as arithmetically calculable numbers, whether through precise conversions or accurate heuristic equivalences. Ursula, a German housewife living in Moscow, argues below that 10 euros is precisely 430 rubles, according to a web-based currency converter. But in her mental computation, 10 euros equals a Five Hundred ruble note. As equivalences proliferate, denominations provide "tropic points" (Guyer 2004: 50; cf. Rosin 1984) for fuzzy calculations and rules of thumb. Rather than generating multiplicity through transcendental commensuration of boundless consumption possibilities,[1] rubles generate multiplicity through conversions, which turn unfamiliar sums—the second category, 5,000—into mathematically manipulable numbers on familiar scales, that is, five thousands.

These three categories engage with different literature and theoretical concerns, but they share blurred boundaries between quantities and qualities influenced by money denominations and forms. These accounts remind us that monies are multiple not only in representing "unfettered empowerment" through boundless consumption possibilities (Dodd 1994: 154; cf. Schmidt, this volume), or through quantitative divisibility (Holbraad 2005), earmarking (Zelizer 1996), or conversions (Guyer 2004), but also, in a more basic way, through denominations and currencies themselves. Each analytical category—5,000, Five Thousand, and five thousands—relies upon knowledge about magnitudes, sums, and numbers from other currencies. Assumptions of one-to-one relationships between economy and currency do not reflect the economic realities of places (borderlands, conflict zones, colonial regimes, informal and illegal markets) and people (peripatetic traders, migrants, moneylenders; see also Fotta, this volume) who have always already been using and managing multiple currencies.

## Five Thousand: Divisibility as a Practical Problem

Indivisible bank notes problematize assumptions about money's quantitatively partible nature. Money's arithmetic divisibility is required for its role as a technology of expenditure (Holbraad 2005). Yet in various times and places, money may break down as a divisible tool for spending. This section examines a practical problem—bank notes that resist being spent—that is not unique to urban Russia and could happen wherever cash is used. These accounts draw our attention to the importance of underemphasized dimensions of money's physical forms—quantitatively material forms of currency denominations—and how they shape expenditures.

As arithmetically divisible money, Five Thousand ruble notes are not entirely successful. Often rejected as payment, their indivisibility presents mundane practical problems. Migrants are not alone in finding Five Thousand ruble bank notes troublesome. Comparing his father's wages as a scientist during the socialist era to his own wages today, Dmitri, a Russian professional, noted that both then and now Five Thousand ruble notes resist use. He mimed holding a bank note, lowering his hand slowly under the burden of heavy money: "A Five Thousand ruble [bank note] is a lot of money. It feels like too much." His friend and co-worker, Sergei, added: "Ah, and you cannot spend it anywhere either." Five Thousand is too big to spend and too small to help with large expenditures, such as rent or an old used car.

Miwako is a Japanese researcher who visits Russia regularly. When asked how ruble bank notes compare to *ichimanen* (Ten Thousand) or *gosenen* (Five Thousand) notes, she described Five Thousand as 'unhandy' indivisible money: "Actually it should be somewhere in the middle [between *gosenen* and *ichimanen*], but usage is very low for Five Thousand rubles. I don't use them regularly, although in Japan I use *ichimanen* regularly, even in small shops ... If I buy something for 500 yen, I can without any problem use an *ichimanen* bill. But here, I don't dare to use Five Thousand rubles to buy something that costs 100 or 500 [rubles]." Although she speaks fluent Russian, Miwako worries about difficulties with shopkeepers, so when she receives Five Thousand ruble notes from bank machines, she puts them aside for rent payments. Five Thousand notes are suitable for hoarding, not spending (cf. Fotta, this volume). Curiously, this is also true at the other end of the scale with kopek coins, which Sergei advised me to "just throw away, or store in a bottle."

Affluent migrants from countries with currencies that have smaller orders of magnitude were equally puzzled by indivisible bank notes. Irvine, an American academic, described visiting a bank machine that dispensed Five Thousand notes as a minor disaster: "So I went to the ATM and it gave, well, it gave me just Five Thousand. So I thought, 'What am I going to do with that?' Sure, you need to find situations where you can use it without being an asshole. But it's impossible if those are all [the notes] you have. So I found a machine that always gives Thousands. Now I get my money there, more or less." In urban Russia, the composition of quantities is a matter of vital importance and introduces new quantitative dimensions to money management. In addition to tracking expenses, wages, and household finances—keeping an eye on the bank balance—respondents found themselves developing unexpected habits: sorting notes and coins by denomination; checking denominations in their wallets before going out; avoiding bank machines that give 'difficult' denominations; allowing strangers to dip into their pocketbooks; and accepting, sometimes even making, imprecise payments.

Sebastian, an American student in Moscow, described a daily survey of his pocketbook, a typical activity for migrants and some Russians: "Everyday I look: how much is in there? Are there enough little bills? And then, warning! Do I have any Five Thousand notes? Worse, [dramatic pause] do I *only* have a Five Thousand? In the US, I don't do this at all. If I have cards, it's no problem." How much money is not Sebastian's primary concern. He has a reasonable stipend, augmented by favorable exchange rates for US dollars. The crucial matter is how the quantity of his money is constituted. The whole money in his wallet must comprise other, divisible wholes—that is, mid-sized or small denominations. Almost all migrants, as well as some more affluent Russians, described managing their pocketbooks thus. Many keep 'emergency' stashes of small notes, ensuring that divisible cash is always available.

For affluent migrants, the 'unhandiness' of rubles draws attention to qualities that were mundane when handling other monies. For example, Ivy, an American education professional working in St. Petersburg, highlighted the absence of usability features for blind people, such as different bank note sizes, textures, and strong color contrasts. Learning to manage cash and coins is not a solitary experience. Cashiers, customers, and security guards sometimes help migrants use money correctly, as Ivy and Urusla recounted.

Ivy: One time a woman was trying to express something to me, and I couldn't understand the number she was saying. She was very nice and very, very friendly. She just reached into my wallet and pulled out a Fifty ruble bill.

Ursula: The total was around 725 rubles. My money was all out of order, big, and small ones jumbled up. I tried to pay with a Thousand rubles. The cashier kept saying no. Then a security guard came … He pointed to a Five Hundred. I never saw it! Then I had two Hundred bills. There was a Fifty in my pocket also. Then everyone was happy. Now I keep my rubles in order.

In both situations, a payment was rejected, communication broke down, and cash filled a gap. Unlike payment with exact change or very close amounts, for example, One Thousand and Five Hundred (1,500) used to pay a bill of 1,345, incorrect combinations of bank notes or attempts to pay with large notes highlight the tensions of participation without becoming a part. For affluent migrants, being able to buy things—provisioning for themselves and their families—demonstrates their adaptive abilities, but this very process also presents them with evidence of their separateness. Although Russians may assist migrants—picking out bank notes, explaining proper payments—these collaborative payments reinforce the migrants' position as outsiders. This is highlighted by communication failures arising from the very nature of the situation that has forced migrants and locals into close interaction, cooperation, and negotiation.

We can speculate on such encounters as conflicts between arithmetic and recursive divisibility. A bank note is presented as payment by a migrant with an understanding that all notes are more or less equally divisible because money is 'naturally' partible. In this view, a bank note is a whole composed of parts, and a payment is a whole whose various potential compositions are not qualitatively different. For making payment, a Five Thousand ruble note is not appreciably different from five Thousand notes, fifty Hundreds, or one hundred Fifties. But the Russian payment recipient rejects the bank note using a different logic: the payment required is a whole comprised of other wholes. Each potential combination of notes is qualitatively different, and some are much more desirable than others. In this view, a Five Thousand ruble note, five Thousand notes, fifty Hundreds, or one hundred Fifties are all equal to five thousands, a calculable number. Although the quantities are the same, they are qualitatively different, and incorrect combinations can be legitimately refused.

In the arithmetic view, we have a conception of a monetary whole—a set—that can be partitioned at any point of the smallest denomination. In the recursive view, there are strict, implicit constraints on set partitioning. Rather than being free(ly divisible), money becomes a medium that constrains expenditure options (cf. Schmidt, this volume). Ursula described a common solution to such restrictions: "Sometimes I buy something extra. I do not want it, but if I do not buy it, I cannot pay with the big note I have." This option—expanding expenditures to fit available bank note denominations—is a luxury afforded those on comparatively large incomes, another variation on Simmel's ([1907] 2011: 217) "unearned increment of wealth."

In urban Russia, the variable fit between ruble denominations and prices, different preferences for specific note and coin denominations, and the shortage of small change create what seem like unpredictable payment rules that must be learned anew at each shop, kiosk, or restaurant. Simon, a scholar in Moscow, explained how he learned to pay correctly at a local bakery.

Simon:  So if I go to buy bread sometimes, it's not that bad, but if I have a Thousand, it can be a problem if I buy a loaf of bread for 35 rubles. Sometimes I have to pay with my debit card because they will not take, they would not want to break, my Thousand.

Ross:  A debit card for 35 rubles?

Simon:  Or sometimes 75 … It's because they don't want to break the note. They just don't have the change for it.

Simon now puts aside Ten ruble coins to pay for bread because these coins are acceptable to cashiers, unlike Ten ruble notes, larger bank notes, or smaller coins. In Moscow, small businesses that accept debit payments are quite rare. But preferring electronic payment to a larger bank note seems counter-intuitive to affluent migrants, who expect small debit payments to be refused or to be accompanied by additional service charges.

The shortage of small denominations is a chronic problem in urban Russia. Concerns in the moment of expenditure over the composition of a payment reflect a future orientation to money quantities shaped by "imagining other people's relation to it" (Yuran 2014: 87). Refusing a bank note is not only about preserving small change; it is also about retaining denominations that future customers will accept. This is not quite the same as Gresham's law, whereby 'bad money drives out good'. Except for a fairly reliable preference for Ten ruble coins over Ten ruble notes, within any transaction there is more than one 'good' payment, as well as several 'bad' ones. As a technology of expenditure, rubles require users to evaluate 'good', 'better', and 'best' payments, revealing a shift from arithmetically divisible money to recursive divisibility, that is, wholes made up of other wholes. Multiplicity is still generated through expenditure, but according to a different logic. The figure-ground relationship that Holbraad describes (2005)[2] changes from being constrained by the smallest unit of divisibility to being shaped by a range of influences, including the sum required, the denominations currently available, and the transaction setting.

Money's quantitative multiplicity is not 'natural'; rather, it is situational and contingent. This section has examined how monetary multiplicity is shaped by qualitative and material elements, such as existing money media, denominations, and conceptions of divisibility. The next section explores how large sums are grasped qualitatively. We shift from analyzing phenomena that could occur almost anywhere cash circulates (indivisible money) to a situation that is particular to people managing unfamiliar money (qualitative encompassment of unknowable quantities)—a situation that is, in some respects, specific to newcomers in urban Russia.

## 5,000: Qualifying 'Big' Sums

For most affluent migrants, 5,000 is several orders of magnitude larger than previous quotidian expenditures, and many interviewees used qualitative means to domesticate these 'big' amounts. The size of routine expenditures is connected to judgments about the qualities of a state, its people, and its culture. Ruble amounts, glossed as disordered or dangerous, became a metonymy for Russia's people, culture, and economy.[3] Exchange rates are also qualitatively domesticated by reading relationships between currencies as relations between peoples and states.

Money's qualitative dimensions are usually considered aesthetically, or politically, through designs that reflect nationalist sentiments (Helleiner 1998).[4] However, affluent migrants' accounts present different qualitative dimensions of money: emotional states and reactions linked to monetary amounts. Ivy described "sticker shock" over food prices: "When I first got here, I had a hard time paying over a Hundred rubles for anything, because just to see 100 of anything was, well, it's three US dollars, but it comes across as *a lot* of money." Like Dmitri's assessment of Five Thousand ruble notes, the significance and apparent value of 100 is too great, yet also too little, for the commodities it represents. A packet of sunflower seeds that costs 112 rubles is both a significant expenditure (because of the sum's size) and trivial (because of its equivalence in commodities). Money's role as a measure of value breaks down. Ivy noted: "I just wasn't used to carrying around that much money, but at the same time I wasn't even sure *how much* it really was."

Ivy's difficulty was not managing money, but the size of ruble amounts. When she lived in America, the cost for groceries and daily essentials—touchstones in a landscape of relative prices and values—was usually below $60. Sunflower seeds for 112 rubles and laundry detergent for 483 rubles go far beyond this familiar scale. Large ruble amounts were initially understood through affective responses: worry ("shock" or "a bit afraid"); reactions to size ("too big" or "huge"); or uncertainty ("chaotic"). Emotions make alien sums accessible qualitatively. The introduction to this book suggests that money quantities are revelatory objects, confronting us with our own, or others', desires. For affluent migrants, large ruble amounts are initially connected with confused or negative emotional responses rather than desire. When ruble amounts emerge as figures connected to such affective states, they provide opportunities to reveal 'truths' through moral distinctions that separate that which is 'Russian' (usually incomprehensible, problematic, or in some way difficult) from that which is 'non-Russian' (relatively comprehensible).

Among some affluent migrants, endless talk about large ruble amounts reproduces and maintains borders between Western 'respectable' monies and morally suspect Russian currency. Peter, an American business contractor, interpreted large ruble amounts as indicators of economic disorder and of social or cultural dysfunction: the Russian people, the state, and Russian culture were judged and found to be deficient due to 'wild' ruble sums. When paying a restaurant bill, Peter reflected on the menu prices and the notes in his pocketbook: "They need to get this money under control—1,000, 5,000. This is crazy cash. They need to drop all these zeros. Go from 1,000 to 1. Reform the country. It's a fucking mess. Get the house in order." Peter's comments are not about currency reform. The 'mess' that must be fixed refers to the confusion and problems he experiences in daily life in urban Russia. Ruble quantities are a metonymy for what he perceives as a chaotic city and society. It is the country—not the currency or the state—that needs to be the object of this reform.

In this dialogue, Peter is using talk about money to create a 'we' and a 'they'. He uses amounts of money as a proxy to discuss Russia and the Russian people, his frustrations with the perceived disorder, and his struggle to understand how to live in Moscow. Yet this critique rests on assumptions about how currency magnitudes should reflect economic order. What is at stake here, beyond moral judgments about Russian society, is the nature of 'big' and 'small'. A menu bill for approximately 4,300 rubles can be used to index social, cultural, and economic disorder only in comparison with other money sums, perceived as properly managed, where everyday expenditures are smaller.[5]

Alongside 'big' ruble amounts, currency exchange ratios were also used by respondents to make similar judgments and to express fears about conflict and projected future outcomes. In Moscow, every central city block seems to have at least one *bureau de change* for exchanging foreign currency: sometimes three or four brightly lit signs cluster together, each with different rates. Ubiquitous, but different, exchange ratios create a welter of monetary values that was described as unsettling or confusing. Jiro, a Japanese scientist who has lived in Moscow many years, noted that inconsistency is the only constant: "There are five exchange rates in a city block, and they change often. A kiosk has one rate in the morning and another when you come home at night. What an economy! Surely something is wrong. It must be dishonest." Fluctuating exchange rates are interpreted not to indicate keen (or desirable) market competition, but rather economic and social problems. Jiro's exclamation—"What an economy!"—blends horror and amazement. We are accustomed to economic and business journalism that diagnoses economic problems from fluctuating exchange rates, but Jiro's account suggests something more. Unstable currency relationships become signs of deeper societal—and individual—problems. Although he may not be certain what exactly is 'wrong', Jiro does not look to international events or domestic economic policy. His assessment of dishonesty is relational and personal, perhaps an oblique reference to corruption. Chaotic exchange rates represent disordered personal relations, untrustworthiness, and the absence of interpersonal trust.

In Moscow's Metro stations and rail terminals, large plasma screens show breaking news and the weather. These images are bracketed by frequently updated exchange rates for rubles against the euro, the US dollar, the Ukrainian hryvnia, and other currencies. These rates appear in the screen's lower right-hand corner, accompanied by green or red arrows indicating the direction of change. The source of these figures is not provided, nor is it as important as the qualitative and political relations they are taken to represent. As armed conflict escalated in Crimea and oil prices plummeted, many expatriates in Moscow—along with financial analysts abroad—scrutinized foreign exchange rates like diviners peering into the entrails of a sacrificial beast. Poor exchange rates against the US dollar and the euro quantitatively indicate an ailing Russian economy, but also, more importantly, antagonistic sentiments between the Russian Federation and the United States.[6]

Fluctuating currency equivalences afford speculation about future political or economic developments—as is expected from financial journalists—but they also become terrain onto which personal fears, worries, and aspirations are projected. As Louis, a French chef who spends several months in Moscow each year, explained: "I have a mortgage in euros. But these Russians, they pay me in rubles. With the war in Ukraine the exchange rate started to drop. Like bombs and missiles, the ruble keeps dropping. It doesn't stabilize, so this crisis will keep going." For Louis, fears about bombs, war, and the loss of his home are brought together through concerns about depreciating currency. Quantities of bombs and quantities of rubles required for his mortgage payments are linked: more bombs mean that more rubles are needed. Currency performance is more than solely an economic indicator: it becomes a predictive political and personal one. A ratio and its changes over time help Louis to understand, and externalize, anxieties about geopolitical tensions and personal financial precarity.

Like bombs, ruble quantities become volatile substances whose value may disappear with the suddenness of an explosion. Uncertainty about the worth or value of seemingly 'big' sums prompts efforts to set qualitative boundaries upon these amounts (cf. Echterhölter, this volume) or to find qualities that help to define and understand ruble magnitudes. The next section examines affluent migrants' efforts to reckon with rubles. The analysis shifts from phenomena observed at the level of a particular social group (new migrants with moderate levels of affluence), which has some features unique to contemporary urban Russia, to practices that are configured by individual life histories, levels of numeracy, and familiar currencies.

## Five Thousands: Calculable Numbers

When money's role as a measure of value seemed to break down, many interviewees turned to technology, including smart phone applications and currency conversion websites. These tools externalized calculations that migrants believed were beyond their mental math capabilities. Based on ForEx market rates, such conversions were understood as accurate, in that they resembled a 'true' value, but not precise, since figures produced this way were not reproducible. During the same day, two websites, or the same one at different times, can produce different results for the same calculations, thus ultimately failing to meaningfully reflect value (cf. Guyer 2004: 30). Online calculators promise 'true' accurate values but provide imprecise results that are never the same twice and do not reflect actual, locally available conversion rates. Eventually, most migrants chose to reject calculations made with online tools, which exacerbated value uncertainties by creating multiple equivalences.

Individualized conversion rules resolved affluent migrants' frustrations with uncertain exchange rates. Such conversion heuristics are reassuringly precise because they are built upon currency denominations and easily calculable relations between numbers, instead of fluctuating exchange rates. In an account of the introduction of euros in Greece, Malaby (2003: 44) writes about the ubiquity of pocket conversion calculators, arguing that regular, repeated conversions were insufficient for learning the new currency. In Greece, learning the euro meant not only performing conversions for payments, but handling, and expertly using, new monies—as Ivy and Ursula demonstrated—cognitively and practically internalizing a regime of new prices. Affluent migrants used their mobile phones like Greek pocket converters.

Based on his professional knowledge, Phil, a young American banking specialist in Moscow, expected market rates to settle his confusion about the worth of rubles: "At first I was checking every price constantly on my phone. I had some pages bookmarked, and I tried some apps. But the numbers didn't match. OK, so, like, this is an unstable economy, and there are different rates across platforms. But the results and rates varied *way* more than I thought they should. So I thought, 'Screw this! Time to figure it out on my own.'" Phil was frustrated with unreliable information about the value of things and currencies. His problem, however, was not the absence of information, but an excess thereof. Johan, a Swedish accountant, agreed: "I had so much misery with online converters. So I had to decide for myself a suitable rate." Echoing Jiro's concern about fluctuating ratios, Ursula noted while walking in Moscow: "There are so many conversions. One here, one there." She pointed to two signs: "Look! They are neighbors, but they don't even agree!" Although individual transactions at different money-changers may be accurately calculated, money received varies considerably. For Ursula, Johan, Phil, Jiro, and others, this lack of reliability created numerical multiplicity that needed to be tamed through individual calculation rules.

After much trial and error, respondents developed their own heuristics linked to easily manipulable numbers, which are usually mapped onto denominations. Thus, material monetary forms shaped how commensuration was determined. Phil's three-way conversion chain used rubles, pounds sterling, and US dollars:

> So 50 rubles is about 1 quid. That's $1.50 US. I was in London a few years so, you know, I'm thinking in pounds if not in rubles. The conversion is 50:1. So

drop two places then double ... that's easier than the US dollar: 100:3. Drop two places then triple. Doubling is faster than tripling. I mean, if you have 176 rubles, well, that's 6 times 2 carry 1, 7 times 2 plus 1 carry the 1, then 2 times 1 plus 1. But with [multiplying by] three, that's 8 carry 1, then 2 carrying 2—you just end up with more hassle ... Well, honestly, I just remember Five Thousand is this much pounds and dollars, a Thousand is this much, Ten quid is this much, Ten dollars is this much, and, well, you get the idea.

Phil 'thinks' in pounds and rubles because an approximate relation based on doubling is cognitively easier than one based on tripling. When he explained these calculations in late 2013, ruble-dollar exchange rates were quoted online at about 31 rubles per dollar. Moscow's money-changers were buying dollars at 30–33 rubles and selling them for 33–36. As for pounds, online rates were about 53–55 rubles per pound, whereas kiosks were buying pounds at 44–47 rubles and selling them at 55–60.[7] Phil's calculations were only notionally based on exchange rates. Despite developing shorthand calculations for faster reckoning, Phil replaced them with a series of equivalences based on denominations, which provided a more concrete sense of numerical values.

Phil's currency conversions shifted from 'accurate' equivalences to precise, but fuzzy, calculations based on currency denominations. Ursula described a similar process: "It happens that Ten euros is about 430 rubles. I remember that Ten euros is Five Hundred, but Five euros is 200, and One euro about Fifty rubles. So 430 plus 430 is 860, but it's easier to think Twenty euros is a Thousand rubles. It's fast. With the ruble dropping [in value], it may even be correct someday." Ten euros equals 430 rubles according to one conversion calculator, but Ursula rounds it to a Five Hundred ruble note. Instead of converting Five euros to 215 rubles or nearby round numbers (220, 210), Ursula prefers two Hundreds. What matters for her is knowing how much the bank note she holds in her hand may be worth in another currency, whether that is Ten euros or a Thousand rubles. Bank note and coin denominations become materialized quantities that turn ruble amounts into calculable, comprehensible numbers. Denominations in rubles, dollars, yen, euros, and other currencies sculpt the limits of known values, creating landmarks for valuation across and within currencies. Such heuristic conversions domesticate rubles as numbers-in-relation. Ruble denominations and sums become meaningful measures of value when they are pegged to a known number in another currency, usually a familiar denomination: 10 becomes 500 because the equivalence is fuzzily connected to an exchange rate, but also because Ten and Five Hundred are numbers embodied in monetary media, which makes them amenable to heuristic use.

Miwako offers a different way to make heuristic numerical equivalences out of denominations:

You know 100 rubles equals about around 300 yen, but right after I came here I converted, like you know, "This is 100 rubles, which means 300 yen. Oh! This is expensive! It isn't worth 300 yen!" ... When I see 100 rubles, in Japanese yen, if I converted it, it costs about 300 yen. But I don't want to spend 300 yen, 100 rubles, for that product. But if this 100 rubles stuff costs about 100 yen, that would make sense. Then I compromise this 300 yen and 100 yen, in my mind, within me, and come to a decision whether to buy this stuff or not. So the unit is 100 yen and 100 rubles, and I started to do this double conversion.

The rule of 100 yen equals 100 rubles obviates calculation, but this conversion is still shaped by denominations and discontent with scales of value. The Hundred yen is a coin whose usefulness is similar to the Hundred ruble bank note. The practical equivalence of these two denominations and their materialization—coin and bank note—enable their new numerical equivalence: 100 yen and 100 rubles can be made equal to one another only through the roles that these denominations play in everyday expenditures, which permits Miwako to rationalize paying more than she would like for essentials. Phil, Ursula, and Miwako, among others, have rejected 'accurate' calculations for individualized conversion rules shaped by, and based upon, money's material forms. Even when ostensibly 'abstracted' as a calculable number, ruble sums remain linked to embodied experiences of money media through bank note denominations (cf. Maurer 2010; Rosin 1984).[8]

In her re-evaluation of Bohannan and Bohannan's (1968) *Tiv Economy*, Jane Guyer (2004: 58) describes "tropes in numeration" as "points where disjunctive values could be linked—transformed, mutually translated—in ways that could produce gain." These numbers connect different value registers and reflect material, historic, and linguistic dimensions of number (ibid.: 86). Traders use extensive knowledge of myriad value schemes to find places where they can make a 'good deal' or marginal gain. The gains that affluent migrants seek are not as sophisticated as juggling multiple registers to find potentially advantageous trades. Migrants are simply seeking a foothold for rebuilding a sense of economic value among proliferating values. Denominations provide a foundation—no matter how tenuous—for precise, concrete calculations because they are fixed sums materialized in bank notes and coins. The value of 500 rubles may be difficult to understand at first, but the denomination and the relationships created with denominations in another currency make this number something that can be grasped.

Guyer (2004: 30) also argues that conversions are "compasses and landmarks on the navigational pathways of currency circulation." The conversions she analyzes are linked to payments. Conversions performed by expatriates through mental math are undertaken to determine whether a payment should be made. Although the contexts are different, conversions accomplished by affluent migrants are still landmarks that direct our attention to 'currency horizons', that is, sets of currencies and conversions (relationships between numbers) that are uniquely configured according to an individual's experiences, money practices, and numeracy (cf. Lave 1988). Such heuristic equivalences permit back-of-the-envelope calculations across multiple currencies. Within the horizon of a familiar set of known value regimes, money's multiplicity is generated through conversion possibilities. Prices in euros become approximations in rubles, with equivalents in dollars or other monies. Each conversion raises new questions about value, but also offers contingent, temporarily fixed numerical equivalences from which valuations can be made. If a plain A4 note-book costs 300 rubles, the price may seem reasonable within Russia, but it may seem overpriced in dollars or euros. Conversion into yen or pounds sterling may make the notebook seem underpriced.

For affluent migrants, especially those who have never lived abroad before, learning the ruble means discovering other currencies, notably the euro, but also the nearby Latvian lat, the Belorussian ruble, or the Kazakhstani tenge. Ivy explained: "[I'm] not just learning the ruble, I'm learning a bigger system" that includes ruble and American dollar conversions into pounds sterling, euros, Turkish lira, and other currencies, broadening her currency horizon. Ivy attributed part of this change to new opportunities for European travel, but also to meeting people from other countries and being exposed to so many differ-ent monies and exchange rates in Russia. We could reinterpret Guyer's (2004) critique of Bohannan and Bohannan's (1968) account of spheres of exchange as an assertion that Tiv, Igbo, Hausa, and Ibibio currency horizons were larger than their own social group, as evinced by conversions strategically made across value scales. The broadening of currency horizons, combined with prac-tical competence in multiple monies, becomes a form of doing money 'well' and demonstrating monetary cosmopolitanism for both Nigerian traders and affluent expatriates.

## Conclusion

The three analytical categories—and the 'unhandy' moments with money from which they are extrapolated—illustrate non-abstracted, qualitative, and con-crete thinking about money's quantities at different levels of analysis. Afflu-ent migrants' accounts of money usage, particularly difficulties using Five Thousand notes and conversion heuristics (5,000), show how denominations connect calculations, money forms, and divisibility. Collaborative payment practices and trouble with big denominations draw our attention to money and space at a micro-level. Such encounters challenge assumptions about money's 'natural' partibility, showing how the divisibility of money is situational and can be constrained. When money becomes indivisible, we cannot assume that this necessarily arises from economic or currency failure: it also arises when actors have different monetary divisibility norms. Indivisible monies and the importance attached to qualitative differences between quantities also show that not all money is interchangeable, as Zelizer (1996) argues in her unusual reading of Simmel ([1907] 2011). Qualitative differences in the constitution of quantities are not about distinctions between two Thousand ruble notes made through earmarking, but rather the difference between 2,000 rubles com-posed of two Thousand notes, twenty Hundred notes, or other combinations of notes. These quantities are identical, but their qualities (divisibility, portability, weight) and desirability are not.

Monetary multiplicity is generated through divisibility (Holbraad 2005) or earmarking (Zelizer 1996), but affluent migrants' accounts suggest that conversion practices (five thousands) and currencies themselves also generate multiplicity. Very simply put, multiple currencies circulate and are accumulated within most economies. However, with the exception of some scholars writing about parallel and crypto currencies, we continue to write about money in the singular rather than in the plural. Money's qualitative and material quantities suggest very strongly that divisibility and earmarking (or divided accumulation) are not the only means through which monies can become multiple.

The experiences of affluent migrants remind us that reports of the death of cash, to paraphrase Samuel Clemens, are greatly exaggerated. Valuable insights for theorizing money can yet be found in analyzing such practices. Cash cultivates payment skills, such as organizing money and finding the right notes to make up a sum correctly, whose variation is about more than handling money or completing transactions. Payment competence (Five Thousand) and familiarity with multiple monies (five thousands) are a source of cosmopolitan pride and a sign of adaptation to local life, even in the absence of language skills or cultural knowledge. As Peter noted: "I don't speak any Russian, but I can buy *pelmenyi* [Russian dumplings]." Peter's assertion puts 'being a part' and 'being apart' in tension. He becomes a part by consuming Russian food (see hooks 2000),[9] but these transactions, in which money speaks but he does not, emphasize his separateness from local people. The very circumstances that foreground being apart are opportunities for becoming a part, through collaborative payments, discussion, and cooperation. However, few affluent migrants have sufficient Russian fluency to benefit from these moments.

Money's qualities are not only dimensions of quantities, as with indivisible monies (Five Thousand), but also ways of thinking with—and understanding—quantities. Without such qualifications, there could be no magnitudes, amounts, or calculable numbers, only figures unrelated to rubles, dollars, euros, or other currencies. The accounts discussed in this chapter raise questions about whether money quantities need to be qualified to be intelligible and to what extent quantities blurred with qualities have been overlooked in consumer capitalist societies. It is my view, perhaps a polemical one, that quantities become money-like, or money itself, through such qualifications. By this I do not mean that a state or nation and its ostensible qualities are the necessary contexts that permit the qualitative taming of money quantities. Rather, I suggest that our engagements with money are not neatly divided into quantitative and qualitative domains. The challenge is to expand how we conceptualize money's quantities and qualities and to study how the latter are connected to the former. Such efforts necessitate attending to the situatedness and contingency of quantity itself.

We need new approaches that are equally skeptical of qualitatively and quantitatively reductive accounts. For example, qualitative accounts that focus primarily on social ties (e.g., Zelizer 1996) can obscure money's role as a form of material culture through which appropriate ways of being in the world, or being apart from it, are contested (cf. Ross 2014, forthcoming). There is a need for further exploration of sensual engagement with money, including its archaic forms such as collectible coins and bank notes. Money is not only a medium we use for economic transactions or hoard for the future (Fotta, this volume). It is also what we imagine it to be (Dodd 1994; Yuran 2014; see also Schmidt, this volume) and how we sense it—through embodied experiences, numbers, forms, textures, shapes, weights, and colors.

## Acknowledgments

I wish to thank Mario Schmidt and Martin Fotta for their thought-provoking comments and Nigel Dodd for his collegial support, which has been much appreciated. I extend thanks to Simon Robinson for our discussions about Aristotle and Heidegger and to Gian Paolo Lazzer, whose conversations about immigrants' money practices inspired this chapter. Above all, I am grateful to everyone—Russians and migrants—who generously shared their knowledge and experiences.

---

**Sandy Ross** has been a Senior Lecturer at Leeds Beckett University and a Sociology Fellow at the Higher School of Economics. She is currently exploring new options outside academia, particularly in policy research. With Chris Swader, she is editing a forthcoming issue on post-socialist moral economies for the *Journal of Consumer Culture*.

## Notes

1. For various views on money and consumption, see Dodd (1994), Holbraad (2005), Simmel ([1907] 2011), and Yuran (2014).
2. For more on the figure-ground relationship, see the introduction to this volume.
3. Cf. Lemon (1998) on American dollars and Hoey (1988) on money and metonymy.
4. For an opposing view on money's qualitative dimensions, see Penrose (2011).
5. Cf. the discussion on hysteresis in the introduction to this book.
6. This is not a matter of reading exchange rates as aggregated indicators of market actors' irrational animal spirits in Keynes's (1936) or Akerlof and Shiller's (2009) sense. Rather, relations of equivalence between currencies—whose antecedents (individual market trades by economic actors) are ignored—become mysterious objects for prognostication.
7. These figures were collected during the period of my research from the РБК Quote (quote.rbc.ru/cash) website, which tracks exchange rates in Russia at hundreds of kiosks and banks in real time.
8. See also Lave (1988) on embodied calculations.
9. On the limits of 'eating the other', see Hage (1997).

## References

Akerlof, George A., and Robert J. Shiller. 2009. *Animal Spirits: How Human Psychology Drives the Economy, and Why It Matters for Global Capitalism*. Princeton, NJ: Princeton University Press.

Bohannan, Paul, and Laura Bohannan. 1968. *Tiv Economy*. Evanston, IL: Northwestern University Press.

Dodd, Nigel. 1994. *The Sociology of Money: Economics, Reason and Contemporary Society*. Cambridge: Polity Press.

Frankel, Christian. 2015. "The Multiple-Markets Problem." *Journal of Cultural Economy* 8 (4): 538–546.

Guyer, Jane I. 2004. *Marginal Gains: Monetary Transactions in Atlantic Africa*. Chicago: University of Chicago Press.

Hage, Ghassan. 1997. "At Home in the Entrails of the West: Multiculturalism Ethnic Food and Migrant Home-Building." In *Home/World: Space, Community and Marginality in Sydney's West*, ed. Helen Grace, 99–153. Annandale: Pluto Press.

Heidegger, Martin. (1924) 2009. *Basic Concepts of Aristotelian Philosophy*. Trans. Robert D. Metcalf and Mark B. Tanzer. Bloomington: Indiana University Press.

Heidegger, Martin. (1927) 2010. *Being and Time: A Translation of* Sein und Zeit. Trans. Joan Stambaugh. Rev. ed. Albany: State University of New York Press.

Helleiner, Eric. 1998. "National Currencies and National Identities." *American Behavioral Scientist* 41 (10): 1409–1436.

Hoey, Allen. 1988. "The Name on the Coin: Metaphor, Metonymy, and Money." *Diacritics* 18 (2): 26–37.

Holbraad, Martin. 2005. "Expending Multiplicity: Money in Cuban Ifá Cults." *Journal of the Royal Anthropological Institute* 11 (2): 231–254.

hooks, bell. 2000. "Eating the Other: Desire and Resistance." In *The Consumer Society Reader*, ed. Juliet B. Schor and Douglas B. Holt, 343–359. New York: New Press.

Keynes, John M. 1936. *The General Theory of Employment, Interest and Money*. London: Palgrave Macmillan.

Lamont, Michèle. 1992. *Money, Morals, and Manners: The Culture of the French and the American Upper-Middle Class*. Chicago: University of Chicago Press.

Lave, Jean. 1988. *Cognition in Practice: Mind, Mathematics and Culture in Everyday Life*. Cambridge: Cambridge University Press.

Lazzer, Gian P. 2014. "Immigrants' Monetary Bank Practices: A Socialization Trajectory." *Italian Journal of Sociology of Education* 6 (3): 153–183.

Lemon, Alaina. 1998. "'Your Eyes Are Green Like Dollars': Counterfeit Cash, National Substance, and Currency Apartheid in 1990s Russia." *Cultural Anthropology* 13 (1): 22–55.

Malaby, Thomas M. 2003. "The Currency of Proof: Euro Competence and the Refiguring of Value in Greece." *Social Analysis* 47 (1): 42–52.

Maurer, Bill. 2010. "Finger Counting Money." *Anthropological Theory* 10 (1–2): 179–185.

РБК (РосБизнесКонсалтинг). 2013. РБК Quote, 18–20 November. http://quote.rbc.ru/cash/.

Penrose, Jan. 2011. "Designing the Nation: Banknotes, Banal Nationalism and Alternative Conceptions of the State." *Political Geography* 30 (8): 429–440.

Preda, Alex. 2007. "Where Do Analysts Come From? The Case of Financial Chartism." *Sociological Review* 40 (S2): 40–64.

Rosin, R. Thomas. 1984. "Gold Medallions: The Arithmetic Calculations of an Illiterate." *Anthropology & Education Quarterly* 15 (1): 38–50.

Ross, Sandy. 2014. "Virtual Money, Practices and Moral Orders in Second Life." *Distinktion: Journal of Social Theory* 15 (1): 6–22.

Ross, Sandy. Forthcoming. *Weapons of the Geek: Moral Economies in the 21st Century.* London: Palgrave.

Simmel, Georg. (1907) 2011. *The Philosophy of Money.* Trans. Tom Bottomore and David Frisby. London: Routledge.

Yuran, Noam. 2014. *What Money Wants: An Economy of Desire.* Stanford, CA: Stanford University Press.

Zelizer, Viviana A. 1996. "Payments and Social Ties." *Sociological Forum* 11 (3): 481–495.

*Chapter 4*

# "Money Is Life"

Quantity, Social Freedom, and Combinatory Practices
in Western Kenya

*Mario Schmidt*

Whenever I conduct fieldwork in Kaleko,[1] a small market center situated
between Kisii and Kisumu, I am baffled by the mutually exclusive perspectives
that *jo*-Kaleko (people of Kaleko) have on money. The people often portray
themselves as cattle-loving, lazy, rural folk who despise money, yet I frequently
encounter *jo*-Kaleko who discuss themselves as lovers of modern life, electron-
ics, music, and the means to acquire these goods—that is, money. This crack
not only runs discursively through the society as a whole, but also appears as
a behavioral trait of individuals. It is not uncommon for young men like Tom
Odhiambo—a twenty-four-year-old engaged in diverse unskilled labor jobs and
one of my closest friends in Kaleko—to openly admire wads of bank notes that
minibus conductors or politicians wave around, but to condemn people's glo-
rification of money in other situations. Loving money, while hating those who
love it, is not perceived as contradictory in Kaleko, nor in the patrilineal and

patrilocal homesteads of Patrick Ochieng and his brothers, which served as my main base during 11 months of intermittent fieldwork since 2009.[2]

In exploring *jo*-Kaleko's ambiguous relationships with money, I do not follow anthropological criticism of money's inherent capability to dismantle 'embedded' economies (Bohannan 1959) or anthropologists' focus on how people reduce money's abstract potential through 'earmarking' (Zelizer 1997). I question the presuppositions of such critiques by assuming that money's quantity itself is culturally important and manifold. Guided by the heuristic proposition that abstraction and quantification are unrelated phenomena, this chapter considers how *jo*-Kaleko make use of money's quantity to clarify how they can understand themselves simultaneously as money lovers and money haters. Moving beyond fruitful attempts to focus on money's quantity (cf. introduction, this volume), I argue that *jo*-Kaleko conceptualize money's quantity in a threefold way: as abstract, concrete, and recursive. This equivocality enables actors to use money as a sign that stands against—rather than for—itself (Wagner 1986). On the one hand, money can symbolize cruel, arbitrary omnipotence (abstract money, *pesa mok bi rumo*, 'money that will never finish') and enforced individualization (concrete money, *pesa mar kuon*, 'money of porridge'). On the other, it is a sign against abstraction and individualization that allows genuine experiences of freedom grounded in the suspension of differences between wholes and parts (recursive money, *pesa nono*, 'free money'). By anticipating the chapter's conclusion, one could thus say that it was the recognition of the multiplicity of money's quantity—abstract, concrete, and recursive—that led one of Tom's uncles to identify money with "life."

To prove its point, this chapter uses set theory and notions of the infinite to frame monetary quantities as sets of possible expenditures. What might seem an unjustified abstraction is an attempt to deliberately translate ethnographic data into formal language in order to be able to compare data across different social spheres (cf. Mitchell 1980). Taking into account that the validity of social encounters in Western Kenya is not a qualitative matter (who?) but rather, as much as economic issues, a quantitative one (how many?), the chapter therefore moves from a set-theoretical discussion of money's part-whole relations to a mereological study of *jo*-Kaleko social relations. Thus, by recognizing the threefold way in which *jo*-Kaleko qualify money's quantity (as concrete, abstract, and recursive) and by taking seriously their quantification of social relations, the ground has been paved for an explanation of the symbolic affinities between money's quantity and social relations, leading to a formalization of the ways in which social bonds are legitimately constructed.

With regard to both the use of money and the establishment and maintenance of social relations, *jo*-Kaleko prefer actions that, while ultimately leaving it open, still offer a preliminary answer to the question, who/what belongs to whom/what? In the economic sphere, this preference for ambivalence is highlighted through an interest in *pesa nono* (free money), which allows its user to imagine an infinite amount of different expenditures as long as the money is not used for one specific expenditure. This preference of indeterminacy is mirrored in social actions that tentatively assert unity with others while ultimately leaving open the possibility of differently constructed social bonds, such as contractual procedures in rural rotating savings and credit associations (*kosalo*).

Instead of scrutinizing how *jo*-Kaleko deliberately 'use' their culture to emancipate themselves from money's inclination to coercive abstraction (Shipton 1989; cf. Schmidt 2017), I thus suggest understanding recursive money as a sign of a form of freedom different from individualism (Simmel [1907] 2011). If *jo*-Kaleko act freely, they do so by trusting others while upholding and doing justice to the potential that this trust is undeserved.

## Nothingness versus Infinity: Concrete and Abstract Money

Many *jo*-Kaleko experience money through its painful absence. Even when money flows into the household, its expenditure is likely predetermined. Typically, part of the sum pays accumulated debts, another portion buys food, and the remainder is probably used to pay school fees. Explaining such contexts, I heard Patrick, by then a candidate for the position of county ward representative in Kenya's 2013 general election, talking about *pesa mar kuon* (money of porridge). In the same way that a sufficient quantity of *kuon*, a stiff, grain flour porridge, indicates *dala ber* (a homestead's well-being), *pesa mar kuon* designates money that secures the homestead's reproduction. *Pesa mar kuon* must be spent for specific goods at particular times—usually immediately—to preserve the household's integrity. Such expenditures are not about choice, so possessing *pesa mar kuon* is like possessing no money at all.

Contrary to *pesa mar kuon*, if a person appears to have a lot of money but cannot account for its continuous replenishment and the moral integrity of its source, that individual is perceived as a *jakuo* (thief). Robert Okiny, also a county ward representative candidate, was described to me as possessing such *pesa maonge gik* (endless money), sometimes called *pesa mok bi rumo* (money that will never finish). Local rumors suggested that Robert spent at least 4 million Kenyan shillings (KSh) on his election campaign, and many thought his wealth was suspicious. *Jo*-Kaleko assumed that payments from dubious business people or drug trafficking were involved. Similarly, people often speculated about how fast the money of Kenya's president, Uhuru Kenyatta, was growing. Some argued that it doubles every day or is enhanced as much as Kenyatta wants. A retired primary school teacher, for instance, was puzzled by Kenyatta's suggestion that all state employees should take a 20 percent pay cut: "Kenyatta possesses a machine he has stolen from America ... it prints as much money as Kenyatta wants. Uhuru does not notice that he loses 20 percent. A teacher who earns 10,000 KSh will." Kenyatta's and Robert's money enables them to buy everything at any time. Their money is constantly overflowing. It can be given away without changing the actual size of their wealth.

If we think about amounts of money as sets of possible expenditures, we can imagine a set, $G$, that includes all imaginable purchases of goods at specific moments in time that are not compulsory expenditures, like *pesa mar kuon*. $G$ contains the purchase of beer later today, a loaf of bread immediately, school fees for unborn children, and other things at different times. Some or all of an amount of money, $x$, can be used to make one potential purchase, $g$, if the purchase cost, $c$ $(g)$, is less than or equal to $x$, or $c$ $(g) \leq x$. The whole set of purchases we can undertake with a specific amount must be a subset of $G$, say $A \subseteq G$, and the cost of all purchases of that subset must be less than or equal to the amount of money we possess $(\sum_{a \in A} c(a) \leq x)$. The collection of all subsets of $G$ that we can afford with $x$, or $x$'s 'expenditure potential' $P$ $(x)$, is thus the following:[3]

$$P\ (x) = \{A \subseteq G : \textstyle\sum_{a \in A} c(a) \leq x\}$$

With *pesa mar kuon*, we have $x = 0$ because there are no possible expenditures, only necessary ones. With *pesa mok bi rumo*, we have $x = M$, where $M$ is infinite or near infinity, so that $P$ $(M) = 2^G$, where $2^G$ indicates the collection of all possible subsets of $G$.

If Kenyatta may buy anything at any time, he can purchase any collection of subsets from $G$, or even all of $G$, without $M$ being effectively reduced. Drawing on Aristotle (1999), we can analyze *pesa mok bi rumo*'s expenditure potential as an actual infinity (a given set of infinite elements) rather than a potential infinity (a set potentially enlarged infinitely but never given as an infinite set). While *pesa mar kuon* is a bounded whole that is already spent for a corresponding set of goods, *pesa mok bi rumo* is a boundless whole that cannot be split into parts and thus can never be exhausted. *Pesa mar kuon* is not a 'ground that registers displacement' (Holbraad 2005), but displacement itself. *Pesa mok bi rumo* is neither ground nor figure, but an encompassing whole in which displacement is replacement. It is an undividable whole—a 'one' without parts—that can purchase everything, anytime. Removing part of *pesa mok bi rumo* does not change its quantity, but taking away any part of *pesa mar kuon* negates money's potential to maintain the homestead. Subtracting a part of *pesa mar kuon* changes everything; reducing *pesa mok bi rumo* changes nothing. The former possesses the highest degree of concreteness, the latter, the highest degree of abstractedness. However, the following interrogation of *pesa nono* will show that, apart from concreteness and abstractedness, money's quantity can also be conceptualized as recursive.

## *Pesa Nono*'s Quantitative Recursivity as Potential Infinity

Anthropologists who have lived in places where they are among the richest have likely experienced the impossibility of explaining their self-perceived poorness. During my stay in Kaleko, I came across a concept—*pesa nono* (free money)—that helps to understand this difficulty. I first heard about *pesa nono* while meeting young men like Tom at political gatherings, which they attended in hopes of receiving money from politicians. I also heard about 'free money' when *jo*-Kaleko complained that all the money they have is bound to be spent in predetermined ways. The owner of free money, unlike *pesa mar kuon*, is able to use it to buy whatever he wants: 1,000 KSh of free money could buy a bus ticket to Nairobi, purchase shoes now and cooking oil tomorrow, or buy beer on

Saturday with the remainder kept as savings. When I spoke with people about *pesa nono*, they often reflected upon such potential expenditures. The notion of free money sparked the imagination of almost everyone I encountered.

Returning to our previous notation, we can understand how *pesa nono*'s diverse expenditures constitute a set of infinite subsets:

$$P(x) = \{A \subseteq G : \sum_{a \in A} c(a) \le x\}$$

$P$ (*pesa nono*) is obviously larger than zero, as in the case of $P$ (*pesa mar kuon*), but smaller than in the case of $P$ (*pesa mok bi rumo*). $P$ (*pesa nono*) is neither empty as $P$ (*pesa mar kuon*) nor as encompassing as $P$ (*pesa mok bi rumo*). Furthermore, as spending *pesa nono* reduces it and we cannot buy everything in $G$, $P$ (*pesa nono*) cannot be infinite in an absolute way. If we buy liquor, $g_1$, costing 70 KSh, our money is reduced to $x - 70$ KSh. Our options are thereby reduced to $P(x - 70$ KSh$)$, a smaller collection of spending possibilities than $P(x)$.

However, given any amount of money, $x$, we can partition $G$ into subsets of goods that we are able to purchase and those that we are unable to purchase. Let us assume that someone who possesses 500 KSh is sitting in a bar that offers ten different liquors whose total cost equals 500 KSh. As shown by the discussion of Bell numbers ($B_n$) in the introduction, the ten liquors, if each costs 50 KSh, could be partitioned 115,975 ways. Our imaginary friend has 115,975 different possibilities for getting drunk. If the number of items in $G$ is increased—for instance, by including the factor of time, since we rarely imbibe all our alcohol at once—the spending possibilities increase extremely fast. Taking into account that we can buy any $g$ at any time we wish because no immediate pressure exists for us to buy it now, the spending possibilities become potentially infinite.

This internal partibility of *pesa nono*'s expenditure potential suggests an underlying conceptualization of quantity that allows parts of a quantity to have the same size as the whole (see the introduction, this volume). Such parts do not arithmetically add up to a more encompassing whole, but, in a recursive move, part and whole can become equally sized. Precisely because both big and small amounts of *pesa nono* enable an infinite amount of different expenditures, they can have the same size: 100 KSh of free money is as big as 1,000 KSh. If $G$ is infinite, then both $P$ (100) and $P$ (1,000) are infinite too. Although 100 KSh and 1,000 KSh allow qualitatively different spending possibilities, both generate quantitatively identical—potentially infinite—possibilities, as long as they remain 'free'. Even a poor Westerner who can barely afford a flight to Kenya appears infinitely rich to someone like Tom, who does not possess free money and struggles to earn enough money to survive (cf. Holbraad, this volume). At some point, I stopped trying to convince Tom that I am not rich. I realized that whenever Tom claimed that I, as a Westerner (*odiero*), am a rich person, he spoke the truth as much as I did when claiming that I am poor. For Tom, having free money means having all the money that one can possess.

Unlike *pesa mok bi rumo*, *pesa nono* cannot buy an infinite set of goods, but instead sets of goods in infinite ways. It is not an actual infinity, but a potential one. Reflecting upon the uses of *pesa nono*, its owner can imagine endless combinations of expenditures although they cannot all occur at once, as with *pesa mok bi rumo*. Returning to Holbraad's (2005) suggestion that money is a ground registering displacement, *pesa nono* enables an infinite figure-ground reversal loop. Unlike *pesa mar kuon*, possessing *pesa nono* permits suspending immediate expenditure; unlike *pesa mok bi rumo*, free money enables the luxury of thinking about the consequences of expenditure. By suspending expenditure and foregrounding its potentiality, *pesa nono*'s owners can enter a figure-ground loop. A typical narration might proceed thus: "I could use 100 KSh of my 1,000 KSh to buy a can of beer [ground:goods; figure:money], which would result in me having 900 KSh left [ground:money, figure:goods], which I could use for a trip to my maternal family members. I could also use the 1,000 KSh to buy a girl a soda, which would leave me with 950 KSh ...."

Like Kant's (2007) aesthetic judgment, reflecting upon *pesa nono*'s potential makes its owners aware of their freedom of action. *Pesa nono* is not conceived as freedom because one can do whatever one wants immediately (Walsh 2003), but because it allows someone to retreat from economic engagement and speculate about what they might do with money they already possess. *Pesa nono* is not only free money in terms of freedom from immediate, necessary expenditure, but also 'money of freedom' because it allows a genuine experience of freedom. Being liberated from spending money on specific goods equals being free not to spend it on anything.

Unlike *pesa nono*'s recursive logic, *pesa mar kuon* functions arithmetically. If someone possesses 100 KSh but needs 1,000 KSh to cancel debts, the difference manifests arithmetically: 1,000 KSh is ten times 100 KSh. Tom often explained that "saving" (*kano*) is "like a marathon." Distinct hurdles signal how long you must continue to reach a goal: one-quarter or one-half. Arithmetically, 100 KSh is included in 1,000 KSh, but recursively, 1,000 KSh of free money cannot be reduced to 100 KSh of free money + 900 KSh of free money. The expenditure potentials of two *pesa nono* sums cannot be numerically compared. Both are infinite. Quantities of *pesa nono* cannot be assessed with exact quantitative differences, but rather through emotional and intuitive estimation. Tom's amazed astonishment at the bus conductor's wad of cash is a case in point: 100 KSh and 1,000 KSh of *pesa nono* are simply different, as one shade of green is greener than another (cf. Piot 1999: 65).

*Pesa nono*'s ground-figure loop, however, remains a fragile way of experiencing freedom. On the one hand, many people never possess *pesa nono*, as money flowing in has to be spent immediately. On the other, the allure of comparing amounts of *pesa nono* one possesses with larger amounts that would allow *jo*-Kaleko to include more and different—but ultimately unobtainable—goods in one's infinite expenditure potential likely destroys the experience of freedom. However, by successfully turning *pesa nono* into 'capital'—*pesa nono* that generates more *pesa nono*—the experience of freedom can be stretched beyond the moments before actual expenditure and made real. How *jo*-Kaleko invest capital furthermore reveals the importance of 'combinatory numerical practices' that will help us better understand how money's recursive quantity can symbolize successful social encounters. Both successful capital investments and social encounters are characterized by being adjusted to uncertainty as best as is possible.

## Investing Capital: Combinatory Numerical Practices against Uncertainty

Discussing financial issues with poor *jo*-Kaleko usually elicits invocations and fantasies about what they would do if they had what they call 'capital'. For them, the English term 'capital' indicates a precise sum needed for an intended project, such as building an orphanage or a house or producing music videos. As a consequence of widespread interest in capital, the sidewalks of Western Kenya's biggest city, Kisumu, are littered with self-help books (*Cash Clinic*, *Who Wants to Be the Next Millionaire*, *Smart Money for Smart Students*), and money-making schemes are abundantly available in Western Kenya. Many *jo*-Kaleko participate in several rural rotating savings and credit associations (*kosalo*), using each one for different purposes: security, savings, or obligation (see Shipton 2010). Almost everybody wants to become a rich person, one "who invests a lot."

Jack Okech, a 24-year-old law student at the University of Nairobi and a classmate of Tom, is no exception. When I suggested that his rural project—a chicken farm to be built in Kaleko—might fail because of unforeseen difficulties, he responded energetically: "One chicken is 50 bob [KSh], when I buy 400, 20,000 ... 400, let's say 40 die, that is 360, each lays an egg a day. If 1 egg is 9 bob wholesale price, per month that is 30 times 9 times 360 ... let me check with my mobile, 97,600. And when they are older, I sell them for 350 shillings each, that is 126,000 ... Some of the money I will lose on chicken feed ... but all in all, why should anyone invest in losses?" The chain of monetary amounts that Jack constructs is comparable to the ground-figure reversals at work with *pesa nono*. He imagines the initial investment of 20,000 KSh—split into 400 x 50 KSh—will become revenue of 97,600 KSh. Once money for chicken feed ($f$) is subtracted (97,600 KSh – $f$), the remainder could be reinvested or saved until Jack can add 126,000 KSh to his wealth ($w$). Continuous investing resembles working toward amounts of the same size—one whole that can be invested—and of a different size—initially 20,000 KSh, then 97,600 KSh – $f$, then $w$ + 126,000 KSh. All three sums function as the same ground (one whole) from which further amounts of capital proceed as figures. Unlike the internalized ground-figure loop of *pesa nono*, capital investment is a successfully externalized ground-figure loop.

However, what made Jack so optimistic, especially since most comparable projects fail? While discussing investments with him and other *jo*-Kaleko, I always felt that sitting down, using a calculator, and playing around with, and referring to, concrete numbers provided them with a feeling of control. Sketching out numerical relations between amounts of money (20,000 KSh), goods (360 chickens), and temporal information (an egg a day), gave Jack control over capital's future application by portraying the investment development as a unique whole composed solely of numerical parameters:

$$[(50 \times 400) + (400–40) \times 30 \times 9 \times 1 + 350 \times 360]$$

The money Jack hoped to possess in the future does not make diverse goods commensurable. Rather, the non-commensurability of the unique numerical whole he constructs vis-à-vis other numerical wholes narrows the purchasing potential of 20,000 KSh to one exactly right purchase: 400 chickens. Through this 'combinatory numerical practice', Jack objectifies himself and subjectifies the amount of money as a unique actor. It will not be his fault if the chicken farm does not succeed, because he did all he could, quantifying his expenditures to prepare capital to be embraced by the unknown, but nevertheless unique, future. He did not invest in a loss, but in a possibility. Without setting up one side of an algebraic function that can be 'solved' by future events, he would have been lost, because capital—as *pesa nono*—has infinite potential. It could be used for many things and must be tamed quantitatively and thereby bound to one specific investment for which it seems most suitable. Capital is thus a sum of money that is constituted by control over its internal numerical relations that are, with the help of combinatory numerical practices, prepared to stand in a one-to-one correspondence with the unfolding, but unknown, future. As the next section will show, *jo*-Kaleko also make use of 'combinatory practices' when they attempt to establish and maintain legitimate social relations. Instead of seeking the soothing convenience of numbers, however, they utilize the uniting power of cultural rules.

## Interpretational Reset: Sociality and Money

After I asked about a new building constructed in Kaleko between my stays in 2012 and 2013, Edward Odhiambo, Patrick's 30-year-old grandfather's brother's son, explained that it is Robert's "office." He asked, rhetorically, if I had seen crowds lingering in front of it and explained that these people "want to make Robert their hotel," a euphemism for accepting bribes from a politician even though one does not intend to vote for that candidate. I asked Edward if he had ever approached Robert to get money, and he said that although he had done so, he would not vote for Robert. However, he added, I should never mention this to Patrick, Robert's political opponent, because Patrick would probably consider it immoral.

Understanding why *jo*-Kaleko often refer to quantitative parameters such as 'oneness' (*kanyakla*) or 'unity' (*riwruok*) while discussing social or economic conflicts (Geissler and Prince 2010: 9) helps explain the immorality of taking the money from one candidate and voting for another. We must examine how the appropriation of money and the quantification of personal relations are connected. A term that Tom used to describe Patrick on another occasion illuminates this quantification of personal relations. A *jang'wono*, a typical expression for a 'respectable politician', is a "merciful person" who, as Tom's grandmother told me, "feels one's own pain and hunger." When asked about *jang'wono*, Tom referred to Christians who are "united" (*riwore*) (see Geissler and Prince 2010) by the love of and for Jesus and are "one with God." Another analogy is the mother-child relationship, understood to constitute 'one *chuny*' (*chuny achiel*). By using the term *chuny* (designating the heart, intentions, soul, and liver), which transgresses nature and culture dichotomies (Masolo 2010: 210–214), *jo*-Kaleko emphasize that mother and baby are of one mind and one body.

Similarly, the concept of *jang'wono* implies an emotional, corporal, and intellectual unity (*riwruok*) between politicians and followers. Despite inhabiting different 'biological bodies' (*dende*, sing. *del*), non-politicians, such as Edward, often conceive of themselves as 'being one' with a politician. Much like transfers of milk between a mother and her child, money circulations between a politician and a voter become 'intra-actions' inside one body. One could say that Robert is giving something to himself: his act occurs inside of one actor, not between many. If he and his solicitants are parts of one *chuny*, it is misguided to speak of bribery (Schmidt 2014). Money is merely being shifted between the pockets of a single corporal entity, not between the pockets of many different bodies. If Robert's solicitants need something, and if Robert is one with them, it follows logically that he must provide for them if he wants to fulfill his needs, because their needs are his. Thus, the main question that people must answer about others' actions is a quantitative one: am I one with the other, or are we many?

However, as *chuny* and *del* cannot be distinguished phenomenally, no visual difference exists between one *chuny* composed of two *dende* and two *dende* that are two *chuny*; thus, it is difficult for *jo*-Kaleko to estimate the extension of their unity with others. The longer I myself tried to do so, the more difficult it became to keep the mental map of circles into which I had attempted to place politicians and their followers accurate and precise. Depending on whom I spoke with, there were many different assessments of whether two or more people were considered to be parts of one another or not. However, many of my informants used the same tool to measure and estimate the size of one's circle, namely, references to what anthropologists would have traditionally described as 'Luo culture'.

What is often referred to as 'Luo customs' (*timbe Luo*) or 'Luo law' (*chike Luo*) becomes, in a very literal sense, a 'combinatory tool' for estimating the chances that someone is one with someone else. Similar to how the establishment of numerical relations during capital investment reduces *pesa nono*'s infinite potential, 'Luo culture' as a combinatory tool reduces the complexity of the question, how many? For instance, referencing the importance of mother-child relations, emphasizing the necessity to be generous and share one's wealth, and pointing out the centrality of patrilineality (as in the case of Edward and Patrick) enable *jo*-Kaleko to be almost sure about, enact, and subsequently exploit the oneness of child and mother, of patrilineal kin, or with generous persons. Thus perceived, 'Luo culture', codified by Luo elders (Mboya 1938; Wilson 1968), allows *jo*-Kaleko to live with the irreducible gap between the ontological certainty that people are one with one another and the epistemological uncertainty with regard to the question, who is one with whom?

The existential notion of the extension of social bodies (*chuny*) is strongly related to several questions. How can parts of a corporal entity achieve a form of agency if they are one with one another? Does the presupposition of the existence of corporate social bodies revive the Lévy-Bruhlian idea of primitive men so entangled with one another that they are unable to act freely? Answering the last question negatively, the next section will illustrate the ways in which *jo*-Kaleko's quantification of social relations allows a unique conceptualization of freedom that is not built upon distinctions between individual and society, but collapses the two recursively into each other. The analysis of this problem elaborates upon symbolic relations between freedom of action and money's recursive quantity.

## Being a Part and Being the Whole: Freedom of Action

Rural credit associations like the Kaleko Integrated Self-Help Group (KISG) illustrate entanglements between parts and wholes in both social and monetary spheres, providing an ideal entrance point for discussing relationships between freedom of action and money's quantity. During the end of my stay in 2014, KISG began a three-month cycle, with 14 members meeting weekly. Their goal was to raise as much capital as possible. New members had to pay an entrance fee of 500 KSh, while other members paid 100 KSh. The minimum weekly contribution was 100 KSh, but most members contributed between 100 and 500 KSh, the latter being the agreed-upon maximum to prevent excessive debt burden for the poorer participants. If someone defaulted on three consecutive payments, that individual would be ejected from the *kosalo*. Contribution rates were unlimited during the first two meetings, a common strategy for collecting huge amounts of seed capital. Fines also increased capital: 100 KSh for non-attendance without an excuse; 50 KSh for non-attendance with an excuse; and 15 KSh for late arrival. Members repeatedly argued that the whole available amount of capital should be lent at each meeting, at an interest rate of 10 percent. After three months, the money would be paid out according to contributions, which functioned as shares.

As not all members were friends or relatives, the procedure included checks and balances. The secretary (*jagoro*), for example, was obliged to follow complex bookkeeping procedures. However, the most important feature—and I was amazed by how insistently almost everybody I spoke to pointed this out—was that all members were bound to each other by contractual agreements. If a participation request was made, members discussed the applicant's credibility. Only after informal agreement on the individual's credibility was reached would KISG's members offer a membership contract. Furthermore, every new member was obliged to sign a loan security declaration form, which required collateral, and a corresponding oath form.

Although I could not follow this KISG cycle until its liquidation, I became acquainted with two other groups that demonstrated how *kosalo* deal with debt default. The members of one *kosalo* had already postponed the liquidation of their credit cycle three times (for a month each time) so that members who had defaulted for "good reasons" could find ways to pay back their loans. The other procedure is *peyo*, which literally means 'to raid, to plunder enemies' but today more commonly means auctioning a member's possessions if that individual defaults on his or her debts. After asking Patrick, who became a member of KISG in order to "learn how to save," about recent auctions, he told me about a *kosalo* whose members intended to initiate a *peyo*. One member, Philister Aoko, had bought iron sheets for her new house's roof with money taken from the *kosalo* for another purpose. Unlike the *kosalo* whose members agreed to wait until everybody could pay back his or her debts, this *kosalo* felt obliged to initiate a *peyo* because Philister had "lied" (*riambo*). Although, as Patrick explained, Philister's husband might have sent her—a common strategy as women own less and are perceived as more trustworthy—the auction was the correct way to proceed. If she, for instance, had used the money for school fees—a "good reason"—the liquidation would probably have been postponed and, if necessary, would have even taken place without Philister's debt. As this was not the case, the *kosalo*'s chairman had already informed the chief, the members, and Philister and arranged an appointment to auction off her valuable objects, including kitchen utensils, iron sheets, and furniture.

As noted above, members of a *kosalo* do not necessarily know each other before engaging in a cycle, as most *kosalo* include individuals from different clans, locations, and families. Thus, members of a *kosalo* cannot definitely know if they are parts of one another or wholes against each other, that is, if they can trust the other members or not—an insecurity and danger that people are aware of whenever they join a *kosalo*. However, I want to suggest that it is the above-mentioned, almost religious importance of membership contracts that sets members free to act 'as if' they know that they are parts of one another. By producing an externalized assurance about the extension of corporal entities, that is, the contract, the epistemological indeterminacy of whether one person is really one with another, whether members can trust each other, is soothed. Such contracts, one could say, are material extensions of and substitutes for 'Luo culture'. However, they can only become such substitutes when *jo*-Kaleko sign a membership contract and accept the initiation of a *peyo* against themselves and other members as a potential. In doing so, they avoid both an outright embrace and a definite negation of oneness with others. Rather, in signing the membership contract, *jo*-Kaleko balance the existence of several possible social wholes at once. They accomplish this by the contractual inclusion of potential *peyo*, allowing for a future recalibration of the size of the whole composed out of the *kosalo*'s members. The harsh and unorganized way in which a *peyo* is often conducted—people form mob-like groups that demolish a homestead's houses to sell their valuable iron roofs—exemplifies the literal cutting out of one person from the whole. By temporarily withholding a definite answer to the question concerning who is part of whom, the contract enables self-help group members to transform the epistemological indeterminacy regarding the oneness with others into a principle of a situationally permitted, and desired, doubt that is experienced as a form of freedom.

## A Sign of and against Life

*Pesa mok bi rumo* and *pesa mar kuon* function as symbols against life's liberating potential because they share formal features with two types of social coercion that are abhorred in Kaleko. The first corresponds to situations where *jo*-Kaleko should act as wholes but cannot do so, for instance, when they are unable to secure the household's basic needs, such as medical care, food, and education. The second type is when *jo*-Kaleko choose to act as wholes although they should not, for example, when Edward made the mistake of taking Robert's money and simultaneously deciding not to vote for him, or when Philister's lie simultaneously claimed and hollowed out the oneness with other *kosalo* members. These two modes of coercion are mirrored in the bounded quantity of *pesa mar kuon* and the overflowing quantity of *pesa mok bi rumo*.

Let us return once more to the notation above to examine these similarities in formal language. To transfer that notation to the 'combination of social wholes', we substitute a situation's unifying potential, $U\ (s)$, for money's expenditure potential, $P\ (x)$. We also replace the set of all available goods, $(G)$, with the set of all potential social wholes, $(W)$. The elements of the set $W$ are established according to the rules of 'Luo culture', which are the principles from which an infinite amount of specific social wholes, $(w)$, can be constructed—similar to the infinite ways that goods can be arranged in the case of *pesa nono*. Anybody can decide to behave 'as if' she or he is one with any other group of persons at any time and space, as long as the specific rules of 'Luo culture' are referenced. Furthermore, the price of a good, $c\ (G)$, is replaced by the responsibilities that actors bear if they construct a specific whole, $i\ (w)$. The construction of a specific whole—a successful 'combinatory practice'—therefore depends on an actor's ability to fulfill the implications of the existence of that desired whole in a specific situation, $s$. Furthermore, we have to transform the 'less or equal' sign, $\leq$, into 'a subset of' sign $\subseteq$, because although $c\ (a)$ and $x$ as well as $W$ are numerical amounts, it is impossible to 'count' the responsibilities that result from the construction of a specific social whole:

$$P\ (x) = \{A \subseteq G : \textstyle\sum_{a \in A} c(a) \leq x\} \rightarrow U\ (s) = \{w \in W : i(w) \subseteq s\}$$

The new equation can be read as follows: a whole, $w$, is included in $U\ (s)$ if all of its implied responsibilities, $i$, can be fulfilled by an actor, $a$, in situation $s$. If someone, for instance, is unable to feed his family, $U\ (s)$ does not include $w$ (family) and therefore can be regarded as empty and comparable to $P\ (pesa\ mar\ kuon) = 0$. The actor is unable to meet the requirements for unifying her family. She is not free.

In the case of *pesa mok bi rumo*, it is the actual infinity of its expenditure potential that equals the endless greed and hubris of its owner. By taking advantage of Richard, Edward pretended to be one with him without bearing the consequences of that unity. Similar to an amount of *pesa mok bi rumo*, a change in their assumed size (from two to one, or vice versa) had no effect on how Edward really understood himself. Although pretending to be one with Robert—even if only during the second when he took his money— Edward simultaneously pretended to be separated from Robert by deciding not to vote for him. As with Philister, he tried to be a whole and not a whole at the same time. In this case, $U\ (s)$ is infinite in an absolute sense as it includes the construction of contradictory wholes. Like the owner of *pesa mok bi rumo* who is able to buy everything at any time, Edward pretended to be able to construct any whole at any time. His non-freedom is therefore comparable with the inability of an owner of *pesa mok bi rumo* to experience the freedom of enjoying thinking about different, but exclusionary, alternative expenditures. As much as the owner of *pesa mok bi rumo* does not care about a change in his wealth, and therefore cannot enjoy thinking about the consequences of potential expenditures inside of a ground-figure loop, Edward does not take into account the implications of the simultaneous construction of two contradictory social wholes that, in his case, became manifest in what appeared to be a spark of a bad consciousness toward Patrick.

Through *pesa nono*'s recursive quantity, money also becomes a symbol for life's liberating potentials. The potential infinity of *pesa nono* symbolizes the possibility of successfully suspending questions about oneness with others, thus assuring its owner that freedom of action is possible. In the moment of building a whole, without pretending to ultimately know its boundaries, relationships between wholes and parts are blurred, and decisions about their size are suspended as they are between two arithmetically different sums of *pesa nono*. Similar to Jack's construction of a unique numerical whole for investing capital, *kosalo* members construct a unique social whole by signing membership contracts. However, the price members must pay is not only to try as hard as possible to fulfill their debt obligations—taking responsibility for $i$ $(w)$—but also accepting the possibility that they or other members will be thrown out of the *kosalo* if they are unwilling or unable through self-inflicted reasons to pay back their debts. The contract's ability to let differently sized wholes exist virtually, in contrast to a lie's actual establishment of differently sized wholes, is a solution to *jo*-Kaleko's problems of ultimately not knowing if they are one with specific others. The unifying potential of the situation remains infinite because the uncertainty of *chuny*'s extension is respected by upholding the potential to reset the combinatory practice of realizing social wholes. Somebody's decision to join a *kosalo* is thus free in the sense of allowing a larger set of actions in the future, including actions that contradict the current one. It is the simultaneous acceptance of indeterminacy and enjoyment of the attempt to momentarily overcome uncertainty that make *jo*-Kaleko's arrangement of social encounters—correct combinations of social wholes—comparable to both *pesa nono* and the above-mentioned combinatory numerical practices performed while investing capital.

Focusing on money's quantitative foundation has allowed me to argue that money has the capacity to be understood differently in different, and even contradictory, social situations, and that it thereby signifies life's ups and downs in Kaleko. Money can be loved and hated simultaneously because of its different quantitative affordances—abstract, concrete, and recursive—that await study in other ethnographic circumstances (see Ross, this volume). It functions as a sign standing against itself, symbolizing both coercion and freedom. What makes money's quantity such a powerful aspect of life in Kaleko is that it symbolizes life's pitfalls and, by being one of the main media of combinatory (numerical) practices, offers symbolic solutions to them. In that sense, Tom's uncle was right when he told me: "Money is life."

## Acknowledgments

I am grateful to Ludek Broz, Martin Fotta, Anthony Pickles, Sandy Ross, and Oliver Tappe for commenting on earlier drafts of this chapter. Special thanks go to Ville Koskinen, without whom this chapter would be mathematically incorrect, and to Sandy Ross, without whom it would appear less Englishy. Furthermore, I want to express gratitude to my Kenyan friends, especially highlighting Heriton Ochieng, who always reminds me that life is much more than money and academic success.

---

**Mario Schmidt** is a Postdoctoral Fellow at the a.r.t.e.s. Graduate School of the Humanities at the University of Cologne. He has published in several journals, including *Africa*, *Ethnohistory*, and *HAU: Journal of Ethnographic Theory*. His current research interests include football betting in rural Western Kenya and the impact of concepts from the natural sciences on the development of Émile Durkheim's and Marcel Mauss's thought.

## Notes

1. The names of persons and places have been anonymized.
2. Patrick's homestead is one of three that are built around the homestead of his father, Josphat Ooko, who died in 2010. Josphat's wife, Philister Achieng (died 2015), gave birth to three daughters, who were married outside Kaleko, and five sons. The eldest son died in 2001, and the third son in the late 1990s. The youngest son, Antony Ouma—who, since his mother's death, has been the owner of his father's homestead—works and lives in northwestern Kenya, which allows me to use his house as my base whenever visiting Kaleko. I did so in February–April and August–September 2009 with my colleague Sebastian Schellhaas, and again in August–September 2012, February–April 2013, March–April 2014, February–April 2015, August–September 2016, March 2017 with my colleague Martin Zillinger, November–December 2018 with my colleague Lea Mohnen, and June–September 2019. While living in Kaleko, I gained most of my data by sharing my life and by 'deeply hanging out' with its residents, especially with members of the late Ooko's home into which Tom was, as an orphan, somehow adopted. Although the data presented in this chapter build upon previous findings and were refined after subsequent visits, the main data were collected in February–April 2013 and March–April 2014.
3. I am very grateful to Ville Koskinen, who formalized these ideas.

## References

Aristotle. 1999. *Physics*. Trans. Robin Waterfield. Oxford: Oxford University Press.

Bohannan, Paul. 1959. "The Impact of Money on an African Subsistence Economy." *Journal of Economic History* 19 (4): 491–503.

Geissler, Paul W., and Ruth J. Prince. 2010. *The Land Is Dying: Contingency, Creativity and Conflict in Western Kenya*. New York: Berghahn Books.

Holbraad, Martin. 2005. "Expending Multiplicity: Money in Cuban Ifá Cults." *Journal of the Royal Anthropological Institute* 11 (2): 231–254.

Kant, Immanuel. 2007. *Critique of Judgment*. Trans. James C. Meredith. Oxford: Oxford University Press.

Masolo, D. A. 2010. *Self and Community in a Changing World*. Bloomington: Indiana University Press.

Mboya, Paul. 1938. *Luo—Kitgi gi Timbegi*. Kisumu: Anyange Press.

Mitchell, J. Clyde, ed. 1980. *Numerical Techniques in Social Anthropology*. Philadelphia, PA: Institute for the Study of Human Relationships.

Piot, Charles. 1999. *Remotely Global: Village Modernity in West Africa*. Chicago: University of Chicago Press.

Schmidt, Mario. 2014. "'It Will Always Be with Us': Corruption as an Ontological Fact among Kenyan Luo." Global Cooperation Research Papers 7. Duisburg: Käte Hamburger Kolleg.

Schmidt, Mario. 2017. "'Disordered Surroundings': Money and Socio-economic Exclusion in Western Kenya." *Africa* 87 (2): 278–299.

Shipton, Parker. 1989. *Bitter Money: Cultural Economy and Some African Meanings of Forbidden Commodities*. Washington, DC: American Anthropological Association.

Shipton, Parker. 2010. *Credit between Cultures: Farmers, Financiers, and Misunderstanding in Africa*. New Haven, CT: Yale University Press.

Simmel, Georg. (1907) 2011. *The Philosophy of Money*. Trans. Tom Bottomore and David Frisby. London: Routledge.

Wagner, Roy. 1986. *Symbols That Stand for Themselves*. Chicago: University of Chicago Press.

Walsh, Andrew. 2003. "'Hot Money' and Daring Consumption in a Northern Malagasy Sapphire-Mining Town." *American Ethnologist* 30 (2): 290–305.

Wilson, Gordon M. 1968. *Luo Customary Law and Marriage Laws Customs*. Nairobi: Government Printer.

Zelizer, Viviana A. 1997. *The Social Meaning of Money: Pin Money, Paychecks, Poor Relief, and Other Currencies*. Princeton, NJ: Princeton University Press.

*Chapter 5*

# MONEY AND THE MORALITY OF COMMENSURATION
## Currencies of Poverty in Post-Soviet Cuba

*Martin Holbraad*

One can think of anthropological literature on money as an empirical rumination on the classical idea that money's power turns on its dual nature as both means and measure of exchange.[1] With reference to this idea, one finds in the literature a series of bifurcations that transfigure the analytical possibilities that this duality permits by multiplying them—a perfect example of what Marilyn Strathern (2011: 87) has called the exercise of "binary license," that is, anthropologists' penchant for deploying "the power of the forking pathway: the moment a relation is created through divergence." The duality of money as means and money as measure is played out in varied empirical contexts through further distinctions that fork the pathway of money in different analytical registers: use and exchange; quality and quantity; concrete and abstract; embedded and disembedded; long-term and short-term; state and market. Even when they do more than just retell Karl Polanyi's (1944) story of

*Notes for this chapter begin on page 95.*

the 'great transformation', anthropologists' contributions to the understanding of money typically use ethnographic materials to sift through the analytical possibilities that these multiplying dualities allow (Maurer 2006). Well-known examples include measurement minus commensuration, where money acts as a measure only in restricted spheres of exchange (Bohannan 1959); short-term acquisition versus long-term social reproduction, where money acts morally to embed rather than disembed economic concerns (Bloch and Parry 1989); and quantification as more than just measurement, where money's quantifying properties act as a register for memory (Hart 2001) or as an index of people's hidden capacities for action (Graeber 2001).

Much could be made of the elective affinity between the binary license of anthropological thinking and the peculiarly prominent dualities of money. The analogy between monetary exchange and symbolic expression is an old one (see, e.g., Rotman 1987). My focus, however, is how the possibilities for thought that money's dual character engenders come together for people on the ground—in other words, binary license as an indigenous practice. With ethnographic reference to the dual currency system that emerged after the end of the Soviet era in Cuba, my aim is to show that the duality of the money form itself, on which the duality of currencies in Cuba turns, has played a catalytic role in people's experience of economic transformations of the post-Soviet era. In particular, I focus on people's pervasive sense of poverty and moral crisis as they shifted from the moral order of socialist distribution—at its height before 1990 and associated with the Cuban peso, the *moneda nacional* (national currency)—to new forms of mercantilism associated with the introduction of the US dollar as legal tender on the island in 1993. In 2004, the dollar was replaced by the so-called convertible peso or CUC, a currency issued by the government and pegged to the US dollar. People often still refer to CUCs as 'dollars', and I will follow them in doing so.

As we shall see, the socialist moral economy (still run on pesos), which has been ailing over the last few decades, is thrown into sharp relief by the ever-encroaching dollar economy. The latter is typified by supermarkets and shopping malls that have mushroomed around Havana since the mid-1990s, as well as various forms of private enterprise that have developed in more recent years, with the controlled retreat of the state from certain parts of the economy since 2006 under Raul Castro's leadership. More than just an emblem of these moral-economic shifts, however, the dollar has also acted as a prime catalyst for them, by virtue of certain manners of commensuration facilitated by how the money form has been deployed. Acts of (quantitative) commensuration that money makes possible as an abstract means of measurement, I will suggest, are integral to the (qualitative) moral discrepancies that people experience in their struggle to make ends (including moral ends) meet amid the everyday dualism of peso versus dollar.

In the conclusion, I shall discuss my own license to extend indigenous binaries (e.g., peso:dollar :: before:now) into anthropological ones (e.g., quality:quantity :: evaluation:commensuration) as an example of the kind of 'qualitative mathematics' the editors of this book offer for consideration. From the outset, however, a proviso is in order regarding the ethnographic materials on which this argument is based. Readers familiar with the recent trajectory of Cuban society will rightly wonder whether it is feasible to treat the period since 1990 indiscriminately under such blunt headings as 'post-Soviet' or 'the age of the dollar', without entering into more fine-grained distinctions that would pinpoint important shifts that occurred in this time. For example, my central idea that people's moral evaluations during the times of the dollar have been routed through memories of a socialist past must, if at all, hold in a different sense today, 25 years after the end of the Soviet era, than it did in the 1990s when memories of times 'before' were still relatively fresh. As for people's experience of poverty, this too could not but be very different at, say, the nadir of the post-Soviet crisis in 1993–1994 and in recent years when a large proportion of the Cuban population enjoys stable dollar remittances from abroad and/or a sizable local income from tourism, state-sanctioned private enterprise, or other sources of income now accepted or tolerated as part of the socio-economic infrastructure.

Since my main interest is in the contrasting moral effects of the form that money takes in economic regimes involving pesos and dollars respectively, I heed this caution about historical shifts by focusing my ethnographic account primarily on the first decade after the legalization of the dollar, when the socialist peso economy before 1990 was still within recent memory and the era of Raul Castro's market-oriented reforms of the late 2000s and 2010s had not yet begun. My material is drawn largely from fieldwork in Havana in 1998–2000 and shorter subsequent visits every one or two years until the mid-2000s. However, having continued to visit the island regularly—including in 2013, some months before Raul Castro announced his aspiration to do away with the post-Soviet anomaly of a dual currency, a goal yet to be fulfilled—I suggest that this analysis remains relevant, if only as a context for understanding more recent developments. After all, the dualism of peso-based state socialism and a dollar-based mercantilism is still in place, even as the latter's encroachment on the former is felt to be ineluctable as never before (Gordy 2006). In line with my focus on the aftermath of the introduction of the dollar in 1993, I begin by summarizing radical economic and social transformations that Cuba underwent in the early 1990s after the demise of the Soviet Bloc and the onset of what Fidel Castro, with his gift for euphemism, called the 'Special Period'.

## The Haves and Have-Nots: The Special Period and Its Aftermath

It is generally accepted in the literature that the momentous achievements of the Cuban Revolution, including guaranteed subsistence, housing, health care, and education for all citizens, were made possible on Soviet backs. Partly in reaction to a bellicose US trade embargo, Fidel Castro's economic policy was from an early stage founded on two pillars: first, export (primarily of sugar and nickel) to the Soviet Union and COMECON countries on trade terms that were extremely advantageous relative to the world market;[2] second, ruble debt financing from the USSR that allowed Cuba to run persistent balance of payments deficits. Both of these pillars were shattered between 1989 and 1991 with the collapse and dissolution of the Soviet Union. One by one, the COMECON countries and then the USSR itself canceled deals with Cuba and began to demand debt payments in hard currency. Thus, Cuba was thrown into deep economic crisis. By 1992, an estimated 70 percent of the country's purchasing power had been lost (Eckstein 1994).

The regime reacted to the crisis by instituting drastic austerity measures, on the one hand, and relentlessly pursuing hard currency, on the other. As a result of cuts on all forms of energy use in the early 1990s, as well as curtailments of the labor force, agricultural and industrial outputs plummeted. This had an immediate impact on the population since many goods and services that were previously provided at affordable prices by the state became increasingly difficult to procure or, in many cases, disappeared altogether. During my fieldwork in the late 1990s, people's most urgent complaints related to the rationing system, which throughout the Revolution had formed the backbone of household consumption. While 'before' the crisis families could live adequately off goods bought with a rations book (*la libreta*), 'now' rations tended to last for only 10 days each month.

On the positive side, these cutbacks were accompanied by reforms that would have been unimaginable a few years earlier. Employing the slogan "Capital yes, capitalism no," the regime courted hard currency by opening up to foreign investors (not least in the tourist sector, which soared throughout the 1990s and 2000s) and by tapping into dollars already circulating inside Cuba illegally. In 1993, the government decriminalized possession of dollars, thus incorporating a significant slice of the black market, which was rife at the time. With Fort Knox-like security measures, more and more state shops opened, selling goods in dollars. When I arrived in 1998, a vast array of products (including essentials like cooking oil and detergent) were available only in dollar shops, or, as Cubans call them, *la chopin*, from the American 'shopping'. This situation persists today (Brotherton 2008; Ritter and Rowe 2002).

So Cuba has had a two-tier economy since 1993. There are those who are lucky or clever enough to possess dollars. Depending on the quantity at their disposal, these people are able to live relatively comfortably and in some cases may even be able to afford luxuries, such as a car or color television. Then there are those who must make do with pesos. In the late 1990s, the average worker earned less than 200 pesos a month (less than $10), an entirely inadequate figure when one liter of vegetable oil costs $2.20. During my time in Havana, practically everyone I met would either supplement or replace salary payments through some form of illegal activity. A laboratory assistant rented a room in her flat by the hour to couples; a truck driver bred poultry in his yard; an intellectual dreamed of becoming a porter in a big hotel. The most prized commodity among this large and dispossessed segment of Cuban society is *el dolar* itself. During fieldwork I became accustomed to hearing the same sociological observation from different informants and in a variety of contexts: "In Cuba today we have two classes: those who have dollars, and those who don't. It wasn't like that *antes,*" that is, before the Special Period (González Gutiérrez 1998). It is hard to miss the bitterness in these words, a bitterness that is all the more poignant since the raison d'être of this socialist society has been to achieve equality through the abolition of class.

Nevertheless, a striking feature of the bitterness with which Cubans view their economic predicament in this period is that it has been largely shared by those who have some dollars as well as those who do not. In the late 1990s and early 2000s, this distinction was just as likely to be downplayed by statements such as "Cuba is a country of poor people" or "No one is well off here." An extract from a conversation in 2001 with a 40-year-old musician, who was earning dollars by giving percussion lessons to tourists, is typical.

> In the times of the 'fat cows', in the '70s and '80s, my salary was low: 280 pesos for a recent graduate. [But] there was ample work, and this was money then. A room in Havana Libre, one of the most expensive [hotels], cost 39 pesos. Today even a *posada*[3] costs more ... Entrance to nightclubs like Jonnie was free; one could have fun for 5 or 10 pesos. At Cia, a commercial outlet, they sold meat ... A pound of pork was 4.50 pesos. At this moment it costs 25 pesos ... I have had two gigs since '96, and they still haven't paid me for one of them.

The point is not that dollarization has allowed those lucky enough to possess dollars to rise to a level of prosperity that was previously unattainable. Rather, for the majority of people, with the sharp rise in retail prices and the decrease of goods available on the rationing system, a standard of living that was taken for granted before the crisis of the 1990s is now felt to be barely sustainable, even for most of those who do receive some dollars. Although the nostalgic image that some of my interlocutors presented of the 'before' times of the 'fat cows' is not always entirely accurate (particularly given the substantial scarcity of a variety of goods during the 1970s and 1980s), even those who fared much better than others in the bifurcated economy of the 1990s and 2000s compared 'now' unfavorably with 'before'. 'Before' almost everyone earned little, but that was enough. 'Now' some earn much more than others, but only very few have enough.

People also made it clear that dollarization has raised the stakes in terms of what 'enough' might constitute. The ever-mushrooming dollar stores now sell much more than cooking oil and detergent. They offer a whole array of consumer goods, from Knorr soups and Dolmio sauces to Nike trainers, Chanel perfume, and other items often worth several hundred dollars each. What I found particularly striking during fieldwork in the 1990s and 2000s was that people would tend to be closely acquainted with prices of products that were entirely beyond their own means. Dollar stores (not least larger, centrally located American-style complexes) were chock-a-block with people window-shopping. After spending hours inspecting the goods, they would very often leave without buying anything. When asked about these visits, they would sometimes provide vague explanations referring to sums of money they were expecting to receive at some point in the future (a promised remittance from abroad or an impending deal). More often, people would use cheaper goods as alibis: "No, I just went in because I heard they were selling some decent crockery in the 'Everything for $1' section"; or, "I was checking to see if they were selling liver today, and then I just had a look around."

Indignation at this state of affairs was so widespread as to seem universal. Whether state employees or unemployed housewives, resourceful black marketers or barflies without a peso to spare, well-to-do white academics with rooms to rent for foreigners or streetwise black hustlers, *habaneros* (as the inhabitants of Havana are called locally) invariably expressed frustration about a predicament which dictates that salaries still get paid in Cuban pesos—the rationing system is severely restricted—while more and more goods become available only for dollars. The fed-up tone in which Gisel (not her real name), a black single mother in her late thirties with no close family abroad, spoke to me about her employment prospects is typical.

> No, I've had all sorts of jobs. With my technical school degree I worked [up until 1994] in gastronomy, in a military unit, the post office ... At that time it was worth it ... one could live off it. But things have been tough for some time now, and I stopped that ... In '96 I started selling flowers to tourists in the Old City, and that was good, but we kept getting caught and fined. That's when I started cleaning and cooking in the tourist hostel for $1 a day. It wasn't much but at least it's dollars. That's what we here call *la lucha* [the struggle] ... Why work for the state, if everything that I need is in dollars? In what country in the world have you heard of such a system? ... Apart from the rice and a few more things, everything I need—meat, grease, detergent, things for the house, clothes, all that—I have to look for in *la chopin* [the dollar shops] or on the street [in the black market] ... It isn't easy ...

## Necesidad

The opposition between Gisel's needs and her struggle (*lucha*) to procure the dollars required to meet them is a theme one encounters wherever one turns in Havana of the Special Period. Listening to *habaneros* talk about their current 'poverty' or 'need' (the term used is *necesidad*, which amalgamates the two connotations),[4] one gets an image of a people suspended in a kind of economic no-man's-land between a half-disintegrated socialist system of state provision and a world of capitalist plenty—of *el dolar* and *la chopin*—that is practically beyond reach (cf. Lemon 1998). This image sunk in early on in my fieldwork during one of many English lessons that I gave to a group of young 'folklore' dancers in Centro Habana. A couple of months into our informal course, I had decided to vent my frustration at the haphazard attendance of my pupils by means of a pep talk:

> Learning English is probably the best investment you can make right now. Isn't your dream to travel abroad? How do you think you'll get by? Even now at the hotel [a 3-star establishment where they were performing for tourists], don't you think you'd get more from the foreigners if you could communicate properly with them?

The class looked stung. One of the lead dancers, who had arrived an hour late, exhausted and thirsty from the street and holding a framed oil painting of dubious charm, derided my attitude gently:

> Teacher, look! Maybe one day we'll travel, probably to Haiti [laughter], but the problems and *la necesidad* are here. Do you think that with one show a week things are resolved? No, I need to be on the street every single day, trying to think of ways to scrape together two or three *fula* [slang for dollars] for my needs. Today I came late because I was in the struggle [*estaba en la lucha*], walking the street since 8 o'clock under the sun, queuing for buses in all parts [of the city], trying to find someone to buy this painting. Here it is. Do you want it? [laughter] No? It isn't easy ...

I suggest that there is considerable ethnographic mileage in the concept of *la necesidad*. The first point is that the everyday deployment of *necesidad* by *habaneros* connotes a distinctively qualitative assessment of their current poverty. *La necesidad* is constantly invoked in running commentary about the difficulties *habaneros* face in their struggle to procure the dollars that they need. What is particularly interesting is the frequency with which they connect the condition of *necesidad* with a notion that has become ubiquitous at all levels of Cuban society (including the state media)—namely, that the Special Period and its aftermath have been a time of 'moral crisis' or a 'crisis of values' (Berg 2004, 2005; Gropas 2007; Martín et al. 1996: 96–97; cf. Pérez-Rolo et al. 1998).

Nearly every index of moral crisis that *habaneros* lament—prostitution and hustling; the break-up of couples but also marriages of expedience; migration to Havana and emigration to the US; corruption; theft; high prices in the black market; alcoholism—is commonly explained as an inevitable, if regrettable, consequence of *la necesidad que hay* (the poverty that there is). For example, when I compared in clichéd terms the re-emergence of prostitution in the 1990s with times before the Revolution, a male friend of mine reproached me: "Nobody likes it. But [prostitutes] know that foreigners will ogle at them [*las vacilan*] anyway, and much better to 'bake the bread' [slang expression for hustling dollars]. There's a kid to be fed at home in the countryside, and no need to tell you about the need that exists." That these allusions are made in the vocabulary of difficulty ("it isn't easy," "you've got to struggle") demonstrates that *la necesidad* is more than just a background condition: it is experienced as something that *exerts* itself. Just as conversations about everyday events are punctuated with stoical evocations of difficulty, the domain of everyday events itself is experienced as being encroached by difficulties that need to be struggled against (Pertierra 2011). To the extent that *habaneros* tend synoptically to gloss this predicament in reified form with the singular noun *necesidad*, it is understandable to think of it as something like a force. In this sense, the concept of *necesidad* is to the social environment of contemporary Cuba what heat is to the natural environment, or perhaps what fate is to the spiritual order (Elliot 2016).

## Pesos and the Socialist Morality of Incommensuration

At this point, the question arises as to why current circumstances should be represented in these particular terms and why they should be represented in this way by so many people, even when the situation for some is less dire than it is for others. A clue to the answer lies in the diachronic depth of the comparison between the 'now' of *necesidad* and the better times of 'before'. The concept of *necesidad* itself becomes doubly interesting in this context. As we have seen, what made 'before' an object of nostalgia for *habaneros* is the fact that in those times state provision guaranteed a relative equity between wages and prices: everyone had 'enough'. Effectively, what *habaneros* longed for corresponds directly to the second half of the socialist principle of remuneration: from each according to his ability, to each according to his need. Or, to use a familiar Cuban word in the plural, *según sus necesidades*. As is well documented in the political scientific literature, this principle formed a central plank of the Cuban state's policy when it came to regulating consumption for its citizens (Collins and Benjamin 1985). The crucial point is that under the auspices of the Junta Central de Planificacion (JUCEPLAN),[5] consumption was organized by the state in a way intended to reflect a moral hierarchy of 'basic needs', according to which the most clearly demarcated were free or subsidized housing, health care, food, and education (Brundenius 1984; Pérez-López 1995; White 1987). Concurrently, state planners made sure that wages in most economic sectors and the prices of over a million goods and services (whether on or off the rationing system) remained fixed from the early 1960s until well into the Special Period (Pérez-López 1989; 1995: 44–60).

The institution of stable and equitable price/wage ratios was from the start heralded by the Revolutionary government in moral terms as a strategy for redistributing wealth to cover the state-designated 'basic needs' of the population (cf. Roca 1994: 99). The moral dimension of state provision was elaborated within a general discourse on the altruistic moral foundations of socialism advanced most vocally by Che Guevara in the early 1960s. Central to Guevara's vision was the idea that a combination of education and economic arrangements based on moral incentives would help to forge a 'New Man' (*hombre nuevo*) in Cuba (Holbraad 2014a; Pérez-Rolo et al. 1998). In this picture, discourses of choice, entertainment, leisure, and so forth, which in Cuba tend to be associated with 'capitalism' or the West, were to be excluded as bourgeois indulgence. As Antoni Kapcia (2009) has shown, this contrast between Cuban socialist altruism and Western capitalist indulgence has continued to be a prime reference point in Cuban state policy and public discourse throughout the years since the Special Period, including current reforms under Raul Castro.

It is important for my argument to pause here to consider a peculiar implication that the state's role as moral (and then practical) regulator of consumption has for the spending of money. In this connection it is useful to invoke an abstract point I have developed elsewhere (Holbraad 2005) that relates to the dual aspect of money as a transcendental measure of value, on the one hand, and an integrated object of consumption, on the other (cf. Maurer 2005; Strathern 1992). It is something of an intellectual reflex—perhaps conditioned by Marx (1990: 97) or Simmel ([1907] 1978: 120)—to distinguish money from other valuables with reference to its abstract character. What makes money so special, one tends to assume, is that its digital denomination as numbers allows it to occupy a transcendental position with respect to other valuables, to stand behind them, providing a quantitative scale for their commensuration. The digital character of money as a measure of value allows it to be implicated in modal 'as if' scenarios, whereby a given sum of money is imagined as being potentially convertible into all the different things that it can buy (see the chapters by Schmidt and by Ross in this volume).

While drawing attention to an important aspect of money, I have argued that this view obscures another one, namely, the temporally bound moment when money is actually deployed—that is, the moment of its consumption in a particular purchase (see also Graeber 2001: 91–116). When I sit here gazing at my pound, I may get carried away and start thinking that it could buy me two Kit Kat candy bars, one lottery ticket, $1.35, or whatever. But when I decide to spend that pound, the 'as if' scenarios that quantitative calculation allows for must recede (cf. Schmidt, this volume). My pound, at that moment, is important, not because it can buy anything that has that price, but because it will buy me something in particular. The moment of consumption, then, eclipses the purview of possible worlds with a concrete exchange and thus immanently strips money of its transcendental character. With possible worlds eclipsed, one is left with just two entities: a handful of money and what it is buying. So at the moment of expenditure, money is not deployed as a digital criterion of value but rather is integrated as a temporal entity in its own right by the one-to-one gravity that the entity being purchased exerts on it.

With this distinction in mind, one discerns a significant paradox in the socialist paradigm of consumption outlined above. As we have seen, a central feature of Cuban socialism has been an ideological fusion of moral ends and rational means, the latter term referring in the first instance to monetary ratios planned and instituted by the state. Thus, state planning is premised precisely on the quantitative aspect of money, insofar as peso scales allow planning agencies to commensurate plural 'needs' with corresponding 'goods' and subsequently to organize them hierarchically within the context of an ethos of consumption-for-need while also considering practical exigencies of production and supply. But the paradox is that insofar as the arcane calculations of the planners remain occult at the point of delivery (the local state outlets where citizens purchase goods), the long-term stability of quantitative ratios relating wages to prices and the prices of different goods to each other tends to render the currency of measurement itself (i.e., pesos) arthritic. The more the state takes on the burden of monetary calculation, the more it tends to divest it of consumers. In the state's hands, the role of money as a catalyst for commensuration is severely restricted, inasmuch as the scope for choice that commensuration opens up tends, instead, to be narrowed by the planning process. The whole point of planning is to regulate consumption. From consumers' point of view, pesos are not endlessly translatable into all the things they could buy. Rather, wages are qualitatively 'earmarked' (Zelizer 1997), since they are bestowed on citizens as preordained vehicles for the satisfaction of preordained needs.

This situation has two implications for the conceptualization of money and prices under socialism. First, wage/price fixing by state planners presents consumers with a paradigm of consumption that tends to eclipse its own quantitative premise, whereby quantitative ratios are deemed as permanent indexes of covalent moral attributes of people and things. In other words, the very arthritic character of wages and prices renders them more as intrinsic qualities of goods and labor (indicating something like a moral 'size') than as extrinsic, and hence variable, price tags. The second related point has to do specifically with money. To the extent that planning on behalf of consumers involves earmarking their wages for purposes of consumption-for-need, the currency for consumption (pesos) becomes less of a current, so to speak. In this context, pesos are perhaps best thought of as tokens that are valuable to consumers mainly insofar as they facilitate transactions within the planned confines of what del Aguila (1984: 89) calls the "moral economy" of the state sector, after E. P. Thompson (1993). Indeed, this analysis fits well with Fidel Castro's repeated claims at the height of the Revolution in the late 1960s that in the long run money might be abolished altogether. A newspaper article from that time explains this idea: "Since we were small we were taught to ask 'how much have you got? How much are you worth?' Then we learned that money was unnecessary ... already in Cuba those six letters (*dinero*) mean less. The new generation does not believe in all the old myths about money" (*Granma* article quoted in Thomas 1971: 671).

Whether demonetized communism was ever seriously on the cards for Cuba is a moot question. What is certain is that the circulation of dollars—illegally from the mid-1980s, with state endorsement after 1993, and then in the form of CUCs in recent years—shattered any such aspirations. Indeed, as I now propose to show, the experience of *necesidad* as a growing and near-pervasive force during this period can be understood with reference to transformations that have taken place in the field of consumption following the partial (but encroaching) dollarization of the economy.

## Dollars and the Moral Crisis of Commensuration

While this can hardly be offered as an argument from linguistic determinism, we may begin with the obvious connection between socialist rhetoric about satisfaction of 'basic needs' and *habaneros*' use of the same term, *necesidad*, to describe their current predicament of poverty. Added to *habaneros*' explicit comparisons between 'now' and 'before', this terminological association constitutes a solid premise for interpreting current experience in light of the erosion of the socialist paradigm of consumption. Thus, dollarization and the new paradigm of consumption that it supports ought not to be related only externally to the 'moral crisis' of the 1990s and 2000s as cause to effect, but should also be seen as an integral part of *habaneros'* experience of the crisis.

So what is it about consumption that renders 'now' a period of moral crisis? The straightforward answer is that the moral core of the socialist paradigm, namely, planning for fair wage/price ratios, has been severely undermined throughout the post-Soviet period, first by a volatile black market in dollars, followed, since 1993, by the encroaching dollarization of substantial parts of the official economy, which also laid foundations for recent overtly market-oriented reforms. As the exorbitant price of cooking oil shows, in the realm of the state-sponsored supermarkets—let alone that of 'the street' (*la calle*)—there is no evidence of an equitable co-regulation of income levels and prices. Admittedly, there have been appeals to social justice in the government's rationale for instituting glitzy dollar supermarkets and bars, since price mark-ups are presented as an attempt to skim dollars off the minority of the population who have access to them in order keep the (peso) sector of state provision going for the benefit of those who do not. However, in practice such redistribution is a sham. People's needs are not covered in the peso sector, so everyone is willy-nilly led to the dollar supermarkets—even those whose pockets are empty. The absence of a significant ethos of equity in the dollar sector is confirmed by the fact that the dollar shops are being set up under the aegis of previously unheard of 'anonymous societies'. Although these organizations are ultimately answerable to the state, they are not subject to centralized planning (Brotherton 2008; Eckstein 1994: 69–71).

Thus, this moral crisis is verily inscribed on the cityscape of consumption in Havana today. The government's media propaganda and slogans about Cuba's socialist heroism in the face of a global neo-liberal orthodoxy are operationalized inasmuch as the system of state provision is still upheld. But the ailing condition of that system is thrown into sharp relief by the ever-expanding dollar sector, with its slick air conditioned supermarkets, shopping malls, and bars. The diachronic coordinates of *habaneros'* sense of moral crisis—the contrast between a 'now' and a 'before' that is more than two decades in the past—are sustained, even today, in a chronotopic fashion (Bakhtin 1981: 84). The no-man's-land cityscape of *necesidad* is a chronotope of the conflict between the past (typified by state provision) and the present (one of struggle for dollars), since the time 'before', when everyone had little but enough, is contained within the 'now', albeit negatively, as a decaying remnant. Turn a corner from *la chopin*, and you will find a queue at a state outlet selling affordable Chinese rice on the rationing system. Look out the window of the dollar cafeteria, and you will see a neighborhood clinic where local residents would receive excellent treatment for free—if there were medicine. The past is ever present, if only as evidence of its relative demise. In other words, the contrast between 'now' and 'before' in *habaneros'* parlance is only ambiguously diachronic, inasmuch as it is also synchronically inscribed in the form of a bifurcated economy: dollar versus peso.

The peculiarly qualitative shift that the concept of *necesidad* has undergone during this period also intimates a more subtle transformation that may lie at the heart of *habaneros'* sense of moral crisis. For one thing, the notion of *necesidad* has undergone a double semantic shift: one of negation, the other of expansion. Negation describes the fact that whereas 'before' *necesidades* (plural) predicated certain moral goods, 'now' *necesidad* (singular) has come to refer to the privation of goods in general. Expansion refers to the shift from using *necesidad* to refer to a limited set of preordained goods to reifying *necesidad* in its own right as something akin to a force that permeates all aspects of living.

A similar double shift has occurred in the pragmatics (as opposed to the semantics) of consumption, which relates to dollars in particular. Negation, in this context, is relevant inasmuch as what was planned in the peso economy of 'before' is not present in the 'new' order of the dollar. But the crux of the argument has to do with extension. Socialist planning, as we have seen, involves as a crucial element the earmarking of pesos as vehicles for the satisfaction of preordained 'basic needs'. In this sense, socialist provision is premised on a curtailment of the sphere of monetary transactions. To the extent that pesos are meant to mirror needs, they acquire a token-like quality for consumers. Conversely, because the new dollar sector is not subject to similar planning constraints, both demand (instantiated in the spending of dollars) and supply (new goods) are apparently allowed to proliferate in all directions. The role of the dollar itself is as crucial to this process as that of the peso was to the socialist paradigm. It is precisely the unbridled capacity of money to engage consumers in 'as if' scenarios—whereby money is translated in the abstract into all the different goods it 'could' buy—that is put into operation by dollars in the Cuban context. Having been placed outside the remit of planning agencies, the dollar comes into its own as a transcendental scale of value that indexes its own potential to commensurate. "In dollars everything has a price," *habaneros* have learned to say in the past couple of decades, echoing their 'capitalist' neighbors from the North. The compulsive window-shopping that so many *habaneros* seem to engage in during this period could perhaps be interpreted as a quantity fetish. The fact that most window-shoppers cannot afford the vast majority of what they see does not prevent them from partaking in the fantasy of commensuration that *la chopin* promote, if nothing else, by means of attractive rows of price tags.

But this brings us back to the connection with *necesidad*, since dollars and need are intimately connected in Cuba by the very fact that the incessant expansion of the dollar sector during the 1990s and 2000s has been experienced as an encroachment on the traditional socialist site for the satisfaction of *necesidades*, namely, the peso sector. As my friends complained time and again, "Everything we need is in dollars." However, very few people in Havana during my fieldwork (and still today) would see themselves as having enough money to satisfy their needs. Even the minority of *habaneros* who enjoy a large and stable enough dollar income to buy at the supermarkets all those goods that at earlier periods would have been provided at a low price by the state have reason to complain since the influx of so-called capitalist imagery has helped raise the goalposts of need. One's reflexes toward viewing dollars and markets as catalysts for the phantasmagoria of desire should therefore be resisted in the Cuban case (cf. Simmel [1907] 1978: 66). For most *habaneros*, dollars and *la chopin* furnish a new arena for an old and drearily familiar pursuit, that is, the satisfaction of one's needs. Only now satisfaction is no longer guaranteed by the state in any recognizable way, but rather has increasingly become a matter of personal struggle (*lucha*) against the odds.

Conceptions of *necesidad* as a force, then, are a function of the transposition of needs out of the realm of the peso and into an expanding dollar sector that renders their satisfaction partial and difficult. In the first move (out of the peso), needs are disembedded from the moral order of socialism, not least because they are dissociated from what was previously fixed upon them as an integral part, namely, the peso price. In the second move (into the dollar), needs become fluid like the dollar, the catalyst of their satisfaction, whether real or imagined. Since the new dollar sector now constitutes the paramount arena for the satisfaction of needs conceived as basic, the fluidity that dollar commensuration lends to that arena is inflected on the concept of *necesidad* itself. In this sense, window-shopping with empty pockets and *habaneros'* constant preoccupation with the dollar prices of goods that they cannot afford may be interpreted as almost *ur*-dispositions toward the growing dollar order. In the absence of 'enough' money, *necesidades* (rather than desires) are kept as the protagonists of the 'as if' scenarios of calculation that dollarization engenders. What makes the dollar so powerful is its transcendental position, which allows it to act as a catalyst for commensurating such unsatisfied needs with a multiple, and potentially endless, series of goods. Like negative *mana* (Holbraad 2007), *necesidad* comes to be imagined as permeating all aspects of living, precisely because all aspects of living have a (dollar) price. If in the socialist paradigm pesos were made to mirror needs, the new mercantilism of Cuba since the early 1990s has rendered need—*necesidad*, the experience of poverty—as a shadow of the dollar itself.

## Conclusion

One could sum up the argument of this chapter with reference to my opening comments about the binary license that is characteristic of anthropological writings on money. The focus of my analysis has been primarily on indigenous binaries that, as I have sought to show, are a function of the experience of a bifurcated economy in which two currencies deploying different aspects of the money form have set the coordinates for what people themselves feel is a predicament of poverty. The proliferation of binaries and their mutual interference have been very much part of this experience, starting from the duality of the currencies themselves (peso versus dollars) and extending to a series of further dualities that come together for people in their own understanding of their situation: 'before' and 'now', 'basic needs' and *necesidad*, rations books and *la chopin*, socialism and mercantilism.

The upshot of my account of Cuban people's experience of their shifting positions amid these binary conjunctures is an argument about the catalytic power of money itself in processes of moral transformation. At this point indigenous binaries have split themselves into analytical ones, and in that sense the present chapter is yet another iteration of the binary license of the anthropology of money. On the back of indigenous dualities, I have sought to build an argument made of further ones. Iterating the classical distinction between money as means and money as measure, I sought to configure with the ethnography further distinctions—between transcendence and immanence, fantasy and reality, quantity and quality, calculation and transaction, and so on—in order to bring into focus the moral and deeply affective effects of acts of commensuration. In particular, I argue that the state planners' divestment of the money form of its commensurative role rendered the peso a token-like index of the needs-based moral weight of goods, and that the release of commensuration as a fantasy game in the post-Soviet era made of the dollar a catalyst for the experience of poverty as an all-encroaching force in people's lives. In line with the invitation issued by the editors of this book, one could see this argument in the spirit of Lévi-Strauss's (1954) 'qualitative mathematics'.

Certainly, if Strathern is right that anthropologists have a predilection to license binary thinking (and in that case it could be no accident that the father of such license in social theory should come from our discipline), then the editors of the present collection and Lévi-Strauss himself, as well as my Cuban informants and the coins in their pockets and in their minds, would all conspire to suggest that this kind of thinking is most productive when it is oxymoronic. The idea of a qualitative mathematics is deliciously intriguing because it is logically aberrant—mathematics is supposed to be quantitative. Similarly, the editors' invitation to think of the quantitative properties of money in material terms is provocative because it cuts against the standard reflex of thinking of money's quantity as a conduit for its abstraction (Holbraad 2005; Maurer 2005; Pickles 2013). Seen in this light, however, I note that the oxymoron of my own argument on the morality of commensuration cuts in the opposite direction. Rather than looking for the (e.g., material) qualities of quantification, I have sought to locate, in the act of commensuration, the quantitative conditions for nevertheless irreducibly qualitative operations of people's moral judgment—indeed, when it comes to poverty, their existential discomfiture. One may wonder whether, as a coin for thinking, money may also be supremely well suited for just this kind of analytical flipping.

## Acknowledgments

Much of the material included in this chapter has been presented in two previous publications (Holbraad 2011, 2014b). With the kind permission of the editors, I have incorporated it into the present publication because of its relevance to the theme of this book and to make it available to a wider English-speaking readership. Writing the present chapter was made possible thanks to funding from the European Research Council (ERC-2013-CoG, 617970, CARP) for my project, Comparative Anthropologies of Revolutionary Politics. I also thank the editors of this volume for their editorial insight, care, and patience.

**Martin Holbraad** teaches social anthropology at University College London. He is the author of *Truth in Motion: The Recursive Anthropology of Cuban Divination* (2012), co-author of *The Ontological Turn: An Anthropological Exposition* (2017), and co-editor of *Thinking Through Things: Theorising Artefacts Ethnographically* (2007) and of *Framing Cosmologies: The Anthropology of Worlds* (2014). His research interests include Afro-Cuban religions, revolutionary politics, and, more broadly, the relationship between cosmology, politics, and other forms of social invention. At present, he is directing a five-year research project on the anthropology of revolutionary politics.

## Notes

1. This chapter was accepted for publication in December 2015 as a contribution to the present volume. I took over the journal's editorship in September 2016 and had no editorial involvement in the review and selection process for this book.
2. The Council for Mutual Economic Assistance (COMECON) was an economic organization of countries under the leadership of the Soviet Union that included communist states in Eastern Europe and other parts of the world.
3. *Posadas* are motels that rent rooms by the hour to couples.
4. On concepts of *necesidad* in Mexico, see Díaz Barriga (1996). For an interesting comparison, see Bourdieu (1984: 372–396) on the French working-class 'taste' for 'choosing the necessary'. For an analysis of changing constructions of needs in a post-socialist context, see Haney (1999) on welfare mothers in Hungary.
5. JUCEPLAN was a Central Planning Board that had been formed in 1960 to set economic, social, and political goals for the country's development in coordination with its political leadership.

## References

Bakhtin, M. M. 1981. *The Dialogic Imagination: Four Essays.* Ed. Michael Holquist; trans. Caryl Emerson and Michael Holquist. Austin: University of Texas Press.

Berg, Mette L. 2004. "Tourism and the Revolutionary New Man: The Specter of *Jineterismo* in late 'Special Period' Cuba." *Focaal* 43: 46–56.

Berg, Mette L. 2005. "Localising Cubanness: Social Exclusion and Narratives of Belonging in Old Havana." In *Caribbean Narratives of Belonging: Fields of Relations, Sites of Identity*, ed. Jean Besson and Karen F. Olwig, 133–148. Oxford: Macmillan.

Bloch, Maurice, and Jonathan Parry. 1989. "Introduction." In *Money and the Morality of Exchange*, ed. Jonathan Parry and Maurice Bloch, 1–32. Cambridge: Cambridge University Press.

Bohannan, Paul. 1959. "The Impact of Money on an African Subsistence Economy." *Journal of Economic History* 19 (4): 491–503.

Bourdieu, Pierre. 1984. *Distinction: A Social Critique of the Judgement of Taste.* Trans. Richard Nice. London: Routledge.

Brotherton, P. Sean. 2008. "'We Have to Think Like Capitalists but Continue Being Socialists': Medicalized Subjectivities, Emergent Capital, and Socialist Entrepreneurs in Post-Soviet Cuba." *American Ethnologist* 35 (2): 259–274.

Brundenius, Claes. 1984. *Revolutionary Cuba: The Challenge of Economic Growth with Equity.* Boulder, CO: Westview Press.

Collins, Joseph, and Medea Benjamin. 1985. "Cuba's Food Distribution System." In *Cuba: Twenty-Five Years of Revolution 1959–1984*, ed. Sandor Halebsky and John M. Kirk, 62–78. New York: Praeger Publishers.

del Aguila, Juan M. 1984. *Cuba: Dilemmas of a Revolution.* Boulder, CO: Westview Press.

Díaz Barriga, Miguel. 1996. "*Necesidad*: Notes on the Discourses of Urban Politics in the Ajusco Foothills of Mexico City." *American Ethnologist* 23 (2): 291–310.

Eckstein, Susan E. 1994. *Back from the Future: Cuba under Castro.* Princeton, NJ: Princeton University Press.

Elliot, Alice. 2016. "The Makeup of Destiny: Predestination and the Labor of Hope in a Moroccan Emigrant Town." *American Ethnologist* 43 (3): 488–499.

González Gutiérrez, Alfredo. 1998. "Economía y Sociedad: Los Retos del Modelo Económico." *Temas* 11: 4–29.

Gordy, Katherine. 2006. "'Sales + Economy + Efficiency = Revolution'? Dollarization, Consumer Capitalism, and Popular Responses in Special Period Cuba." *Public Culture* 18 (2): 383–412.

Graeber, David. 2001. *Toward an Anthropological Theory of Value: The False Coin of Our Own Dreams.* New York: Palgrave.

Gropas, Maria. 2007. "The Repatriotization of Revolutionary Ideology and Mnemonic Landscape in Present-Day Havana." *Current Anthropology* 48 (4): 531–549.

Haney, Lynne. 1999. "'But We Are Still Mothers': Gender, the State, and the Construction of Need in Postsocialist Hungary." In *Uncertain Transition: Ethnographies of Change in the Postsocialist World*, ed. Michael Burawoy and Katherine Verdery, 151–188. Lanham, MD: Rowman & Littlefield.

Hart, Keith. 2001. *Money in an Unequal World.* New York: Texere.

Holbraad, Martin. 2005. "Expending Multiplicity: Money in Cuban Ifá Cults." *Journal of the Royal Anthropological Institute* 11 (2): 231–254.

Holbraad, Martin. 2007. "The Power of Powder: Multiplicity and Motion in the Divinatory Cosmology of Cuban Ifá (or *Mana* Again)." In *Thinking Through Things: Theorising Artefacts Ethnographically*, ed. Amiria Henare, Martin Holbraad, and Sari Wastell, 189–225. London: Routledge.

Holbraad, Martin. 2011. "Dinheiro e Necessidades no 'Period Especial' de Havana." In *Outras Ilhas: Espaços, Temporalidades e Transformações em Cuba*, ed. Olívia Maria Gomez da Cunha, 367–394. Rio de Janeiro: Aeroplano Etitora.

Holbraad, Martin. 2014a. "*Revolución o Muerte*: The Political Ontology of Cuban Revolution." *Ethnos* 79 (3): 365–387.

Holbraad, Martin. 2014b. "The Values of Money: Economies of Need in Contemporary Cuba." *Suomen Antropologi* 39 (2): 5–19.

Kapcia, Antoni. 2009. "Lessons of the Special Period: Learning to March Again." *Latin American Perspectives* 36 (1): 30–41.

Lemon, Alaina. 1998. "'Your Eyes Are Green Like Dollars': Counterfeit Cash, National Substance, and Currency Apartheid in 1990s Russia." *Cultural Anthropology* 13 (1): 22–55.

Lévi-Strauss, Claude. 1954. "Introduction: The Mathematics of Man." *International Social Science Bulletin* 6 (4): 581–590.

Martín, Consuelo, Maricela Perera, and Maiky Díaz. 1996. "La Vida Cotidiana en Cuba: Una Mirada Psicosocial." *Revista Temas* 7: 92–98.

Marx, Karl. 1990. *Capital: A Critique of Political Economy, Volume 1*. Trans. Ben Fowkes. London: Penguin.

Maurer, Bill. 2005. "Does Money Matter? Abstraction and Substitution in Alternative Financial Forms." In *Materiality*, ed. Daniel Miller, 140–164. Durham, NC: Duke University Press.

Maurer, Bill. 2006. "The Anthropology of Money." *Annual Review of Anthropology* 35: 15–36.

Pérez-López, Jorge F. 1989. "Wages, Earnings, Hours of Work, and Retail Prices in Cuba." *Cuban Studies* 19: 199–224.

Pérez-López, Jorge F. 1995. *Cuba's Second Economy: From Behind the Scenes to Center Stage*. New Brunswick, NJ: Transaction.

Pérez-Rolo, Martha, Juan A. Blanco, Miguel Limia, Delia L. López, and Jonathán Quirós. 1998. "El Socialismo y el Hombre en Cuba: Una Mirada en los 90." *Temas* 11: 105–119.

Pertierra, Anna C. 2011. *Cuba: The Struggle for Consumption*. Pompano Beach, FL: Caribbean Studies Press.

Pickles, Anthony J. 2013. "Pocket Calculator: A Humdrum 'Obviator' in Papua New Guinea?" *Journal of the Royal Anthropological Institute* 19 (3): 510–526.

Polanyi, Karl. 1944. *The Great Transformation: The Political and Economic Origins of Our Time*. Boston: Beacon Press.

Ritter, Archibald R. M., and Nicholas Rowe. 2002. "Cuba: From 'Dollarization' to 'Euroization' or 'Peso Reconsolidation'?" *Latin American Politics and Society* 44 (2): 99–123.

Roca, Sergio G. 1994. "Reflections on Economic Policy: Cuba's Food Program." In *Cuba at a Crossroads: Politics and Economics after the 4th Party Congress*, ed. Jorge F. Pérez-López, 94–117. Gainesville: University Press of Florida.

Rotman, Brian. 1987. *Signifying Nothing: The Semiotics of Zero*. Stanford, CA: Stanford University Press.

Simmel, Georg. (1907) 1978. *The Philosophy of Money*. Trans. Tom Bottomore and David Frisby. London: Routledge.

Strathern, Marilyn. 1992. "Qualified Value: The Perspective of Gift Exchange." In *Barter, Exchange and Value: An Anthropological Approach*, ed. Caroline Humphrey and Stephen Hugh-Jones, 169–191. Cambridge: Cambridge University Press.

Strathern, Marilyn. 2011. "Binary License." *Common Knowledge* 17 (1): 87–103.

Thomas, Hugh. 1971. *The Cuban Revolution*. New York: Harper & Row.

Thompson, E. P. 1993. *Customs in Common: Studies in Traditional Popular Culture*. New York: New Press.

White, Gordon. 1987. "Cuban Planning in the Mid-1980s: Centralization, Decentralization, and Participation." *World Development* 15 (1): 153–161.

Zelizer, Viviana A. 1997. *The Social Meaning of Money: Pin Money, Paychecks, Poor Relief, and Other Currencies*. Princeton, NJ: Princeton University Press.

*Chapter 6*

# 'MONEY ON THE STREET' AS A HOARD
## How Informal Moneylenders Remain Unbanked

*Martin Fotta*

In Bahia, northeast Brazil, Calon Gypsy settlements are composed of bilaterally related people and emerge around particularly influential men. Generally, settlements are located on the outskirts of towns or in peripheral neighborhoods, and there is a high level of mobility, with the exception of settlements' 'strongmen' and their families. A strongman is considered 'strong' (*forte*) by other Calon and 'established' (*estabelecido*) in a particular region. He has good relations with local authorities and much money in loans to Jurons (non-Gypsies). His reputation lends social capital and support to households associated with him.

In São Gabriel, one such tent settlement was located on a small hill close to a town entrance. Its strongman, nicknamed 'Vaqueiro' (Cowboy), rented the land and arranged electricity and water from a Juron neighbor. In the eyes of other Calon, Vaqueiro was a *ganhador*, that is, one who gains, a (bread)winner. He lived with Sara, and for both this was their second marriage. As he did not

Notes for this chapter begin on page 112.

have children on his own and his close relatives lived elsewhere, most house-holds of the settlement—on average about seven tents occupied by nuclear families—were of Sara's siblings and their children.

When Vaqueiro died in the summer of 2012, the settlement fell apart. People left within three days of his death, since, as his nephew explained to me, "Ciga-nos [Gypsies] do not stay living where somebody has died." Most households ended up in an improvised camp next to a busy interstate. I visited them a few weeks later, first entering a tent of Sara's older sister and her husband; their son's tent was next to theirs. Immediately, Sara's sister reported on Vaqueiro's death: "It was so sudden. Nobody knows why. He was not ill. He had diabetes, but diabetes does not kill. His head hurt in the morning, a vein on his neck swelled up. He got a headache and it got into his brain ... They [Sara and her son-in-law] took him to Salvador. He was there for several days. But his brain did not work anymore. His heart still beat, because he had a strong heart ... They spent fifteen thousand [Brazilian reals] ... My sister broke up everything. She burnt the bed and the tent. She sold the fridge and the stove."

A few days later, I went to see Sara, who was then living in a house rented by Jair, her son-in-law. I found her sitting under a tree, dressed in a simple dark blue dress, her hair tied up in a messy bun. She started crying: "Everything reminds me of my deceased *companheiro*." Because she continued residing in the same town, she explained, she could not even walk out of her house with-out remembering him. According to Sara, the most terrible thing was that "his death could not be explained" as he had not been ill. "The man left the house in the morning, and one hour later he was dead," she continued, stating how much money his treatment had cost: R$3,000 for the ambulance transport to Cachoeira and R$5,000 for an intensive care unit in Salvador.

All people close to Vaqueiro willingly shared exact sums spent on saving him. The sums almost invariably diverged, and even Sara might have reasons for exaggerating or diminishing them. Usually, I was also informed how Sara broke up the couple's bed and threw out and burned some contents of their tent. Her children sold the rest. Without a husband or money of her own, Sara became dependent on others for support, primarily Jair, who inherited Vaqueiro's promissory notes (*letras*). On that basis, he later collected money from Vaqueiro's debtors—both Juron and Calon. Vaqueiro's debts to other Calon, however, were never to be paid off. By taking over Vaqueiro's debtors (and money), Jair established himself more firmly in the town. Four years after Vaqueiro's death, a small settlement had grown up around him; he and his wife's cousin had constructed modest houses, while Sara and her sister, with her husband, lived in tents on their children's property. Although Jair was criti-cized by some relatives as "constantly crying about [the lack of] money," they did not consider him poor.

On the one hand, what I describe here sounds familiar to the student of the anthropology of Romani communities (Gypsies). Property destruction and avoidance of places associated with the dead have been tied to mourning pro-cesses, as well as inheritance attitudes in the scholarly literature (e.g., Manrique 2016; Vilar 2016; Williams 2003). On the other hand, I was perplexed. Here were the people who had just abandoned their settlement and were living in a muddy camp next to an illegal dump, yet they seemed uninterested in discussing this radical change. Instead, everyone, including Sara, readily offered information to visitors about sums spent saving Vaqueiro and about what Sara and her children did with the couple's property and money.

Admittedly, Calon's money-talk could be approached as reflecting commodification of interpersonal relations and calculability of sentiments in the wake of the growing importance of financial institutions in, and the increasing monetization of, the day-to-day life in the Brazilian hinterland. From this angle, it would appear unsurprising that Calon, who specialize as moneylenders and are fully immersed in the current credit economy, resort to enumeration (of money or valuable objects) to express the worth of people and social relations. Although this line of argumentation is tempting, I want to suggest almost the contrary: that this mathematical discourse points to the suspension of calculation in a process that makes relationships between people and their continued commitment to Calon morality visible. The fact is that everybody I talked to also held some idea of how much money Vaqueiro and Jair had in circulation and how much money the latter had inherited and added to his wealth. Furthermore, everybody related these sums to the men's 'strength', an attribute of their social personhood that became materialized in the emergency cash Jair amassed to save Vaqueiro and which thus objectified the former's creditability. All transactions circle around such 'money on the street' (*dinheiro na rua*), from which sums involved are seen as being displaced or which they co-constitute as an aspect of each man's unique life-world. And because money on the street is a subject of others' claims and desires, any expenditure—always a precise sum—is potentially worth discussing which realizes an individual's community simultaneously with the encompassment of this whole—a vague but specific summation—by Calon values. Far from signaling submission to the financialized regime and abstraction from social relationships through money, this 'number ecology' (Day et al. 2014), which participates in composing a form of life, is a declaration of Calon autonomy vis-à-vis the rest of the world.

To substantiate these claims, I bring together two main strands. First, I follow Gustav Peebles's (2014) call to take 'unbanking' seriously, arguing that money on the street pertaining to any individual is best approached as a 'hoard' that orients subjectivities and serves as an anchor point for communal life (cf. Seitz, this volume). Second, I draw on Martin Holbraad's (2005: 245) conceptualization of the "quantitative quality," or 'quality of multiplicity', that attends to money as a technology of expenditure and movement. When we seriously consider Calon's focus on the displacement of sums from composite hoards, which are brought into being through men's actions, we realize that even if, in some ways, Calon create a society where life seems accounted for, enumeration enacts deaths and other events as unpredictable, or highlights them as singular outcomes of individuals' efforts. To borrow, somewhat frivolously, from a philosopher: mathematization, which allows us to say more about the world than we would otherwise be able to, can in this case be said to "effect a liberation from the limits of calculatory reason" (Meillassoux 2008: 103). It makes the unfolding of social life unaccountable, in that events can appear as unrelated (and 'non-relating') to one another, be it the financial logic of moneymaking loans or some transcendental cultural register.

Like other marginalized people who 'live for the moment' (Day et al. 1998), Gypsies have been characterized as failing "to follow the state's dominant 'future orientation'" (Peebles 2008: 234n2). In doing so, they thus maintain their often precarious sovereignty from the surrounding majority society (and its state). Anthropologists have noted the role that complicating and hybridizing money's capacity for commensuration and the homogenization of values have played in maintaining the distinctiveness of Romani communities (e.g., Olivera 2016; Stewart 1994). It is therefore necessary to briefly discuss these ethnographies and to highlight the specificity of the mode of life that I discuss here.

## Gypsy Money

According to Michael Stewart (1994, 1997), for Hungarian Vlach Rom, money becomes problematic because it makes visible tensions between household interests and the egalitarian ideology of brotherhood. He argues that Rom men disengage money from more powerful Gažos (non-Gypsies) and from demands of their households in different moments: in horse market deals representing *Romani butji* (Romani trades/work), where men circulate factory-earned wages or money from women's pig husbandry; in gambling, where Gažo-tainted money is almost ritually cleaned; or in merrymaking among 'brothers', where money is spent. In these contexts, Rom men present an image of a world of abundance, freed from reproductive demands, where positive qualities of themselves as Rom are foregrounded. In the process, money is turned from Gažo money (Hungarian forints) as a limited good, earned in factories or spent within households, into money as bountiful silver or pengö.[1] Money becomes a medium for expressing ideals of sharing between Rom and for subverting power relations between Rom and Gažos. It seems to flow easily from Gažos toward lucky (*baxtale*), true Rom. As 'liquid' wealth, it is valued for its quality of "brute quantity as physical object of red and green cash money" (Stewart 1994: 57).[2]

For Stewart, this resignification of money is a reaction to Rom marginality in Hungarian society. Martin Olivera (2016), however, finds this line of argumentation limiting because it approaches money through the prism of scarcity, in a Gažo manner. This results in seeing accumulation and household continuity, as opposed to sharing, and in reducing abundance to the mystification of money's essential scarcity. Olivera shows how, among the Gabori of Romania, the money from *Romani butji* is always already spent, even before it is earned. Symmetrically, Gabori view this money as always earnable, as non-scarce. If Gabori see themselves as 'lucky', it is not because they believe in a 'free lunch', but because monies are qualitatively different. Money earned in *Romani butji* is characterized by use value rather than exchange value, and differs from money made through 'women's work'. While the latter guarantees the physical survival of households, the former is earned to meet specific social goals, such as financing a wedding. Given these qualities, *Romani butji* money does not raise a specter of commensuration between domains. It is not only always there—produced by Gaźos as a materialization of exchange value—but also always already encompassed by Gabori ethics.

While I am sympathetic to Olivera's critique, it misses a critical point in Stewart's analysis: how money, in the form of state currency, needs to be detached from the state and its project of shaping individual subjectivities and communities. This becomes clear when comparing descriptions of domestic economy from each case. In both instances, women or 'women's work' (which could be done by men) provides subsistence for the household. In the Gabori case, money from *Romani butji* can also be used for house reconstruction. In contrast, Stewart suggests that, for Vlach Rom, money made through horse trade is always preferentially spent on new horses. The difference becomes understandable when we consider that during state socialism, Vlach Rom households and their interests could be hijacked by the assimilating state. Rom families became primary sites for turning 'Gypsies' into citizen-laborers by, for example, providing low-interest loans or housing to newlyweds. The accentuated ethics of brotherhood and practices such as sharing—subsumed under the term *Romanes* (a Rom way of doing things)—served as "communal devices to protect themselves" (Stewart 1994: 55). Similar concerns are not present among Gabori of the post-socialist era, whose experiences were characterized by cross-border mobility and by a multiplicity of currencies, where familial reproduction was not tied up closely with state-enforced employment and its system of redistribution.

Like these two communities, the Bahian Calon I came to know best—a network of about 150 households living in five neighboring municipalities—view their interest in money as legitimate. Money and ways of making and spending it are constantly discussed, while the possibility of concealing money in a bank or divulging knowledge about one's loans gives rise to lively debates about people's behavior. Specific sums and attitudes toward money become accessible forms for talking about relationships between people: money infuses the character of households, settlements, and events, such as weddings or acts of violence. Money becomes a technology for fabricating Calon life-worlds in the midst of non-Gypsies. However, this is not only, or even primarily, effected through individual exchanges of different modalities that reflect differentiated morality. While these 'qualifications' of money are certainly important (see Fotta 2016b), I suggest bracketing these analytically and starting with what dominates Calon conversations: composites of all the money that individual men have 'in circulation', and the exact sums involved in transactions that are somehow linked to them. If the Vlach Rom and Gabori ethnographies reveal that the main preoccupation of various Romani communities is "the danger of disintegration" of their communal lives (Williams 1982: 335), for Calon, the continuity of proper sociality is at least partly guaranteed by the potential visibility of each man's money on the street to significant others and the possibility of marking this hoard numerically.

## Calon Hoards

Like other populations of service providers, Ciganos (Gypsies) of Brazil have always been immersed in commercial economies mediated by money. In the nineteenth century, they were known as peripatetic traders of slaves and animals and, to a lesser degree, as moneylenders. Since most trade was done on credit, these two activities were connected. In Bahia today, Calon are commonly seen as moneylenders (*agiotas*). An anthropologist reports on non-Gypsies referring to Gypsies as an "informal bank" (Thiele 2008: 144), and a journalist writing about credit opportunities for peasants describes them as "bankers of the hinterland" (Billi 2005). As in the past, Calon exploit possibilities for arbitrage: across distance in trans-local trade, and across time in moneylending. Today, as in the past, such possibilities belong to a milieu within which state and other authorities impose borders, regulations, and formalities that shape the character of locally sanctioned debts.

As the primary occupation of Calon, moneylending arose in a recent era when, stimulated by the state's policies, over a very short period huge sectors of the Brazilian population were incorporated into the financial service market (e.g., Müller 2014). If household consumption was the major motor of Brazilian economic growth under the Workers' Party governments between 2003 and 2016, it was ultimately enabled by the radical increase and expansion of the credit supply. When those who overcame the threshold of poverty and joined the expanded labor market could not meet their financial obligations, they often turned to moneylenders. Almost invariably, they used bank or welfare benefit cards or pre-dated checks—state-authorized technologies of formalized monetary flow—as collateral. Local politicians and incumbents sometimes borrowed money from moneylenders to finance their campaigns, using federal transfers or municipal property in the same way.

The state's role in shaping this market is crucial. When classical sociologists treated the growing abstraction and homogenization of social life through reducing all distinctive values to one medium of money, as almost a natural consequence of its properties, they commonly misrecognized the role of nation-states in the dynamics they observed (Gilbert 2005). The rise of national currencies in the nineteenth century and their pegging to gold undeniably shaped their accounts of money's impact on social life. However, as Peebles (2008) points out, the same period also saw the spread of formal banking, in which people's money stuffed in mattresses was turned into savings by being brought to local banks, which began to circulate credit and paper currency backed up by this general reserve. This movement transferred responsibility for individuals' future planning to official institutions, rearranged community boundaries, and reoriented subjectivities. People started experiencing themselves as part of their national economy, not only because of the specific nation's currency that bound them imaginatively through iconography and circulation within national borders, but also because each individual's new relationships of credit and debt were oriented by a new material whole: the national reserve. Peebles suggests treating this reserve as a hoard—now shared with other citizens as an aggregate of their savings—and in so doing enables comparisons with hoards of classic ethnographic records. The latter, as hidden sources of power, allowed their owners to act within their communities, which in fact emerged in the act of recognizing the hoards' existence (see also Peebles 2014).

The broad contours of the dynamics Peebles describes resonate with the processes of 'banking the unbanked', 'financial inclusion', and 'social inclusion through the market', by which financial mechanisms and instruments were expanded to those Brazilians who until recently did not have access to them. However, there exist Brazilians who, despite their full participation within this economic system, have 'domesticated' financialization and, in so doing, have reinvented their resilience and separateness from others. I suggest that Calon of Bahia refuse to treat the state as the final arbiter of value and refuse to tie their future to it, despite the fact that they use a whole range of new, formal financial services and seek out opportunities within the expanding credit economy. Although they make a living through circulating money in the form of loans, they do not treat money as abstract or the monetary sphere as transcendent. Rather, the continued distinctiveness of Calon, despite their dependence on Jurons for subsistence and their utilization of formal financial products, is premised on Calon treatment of money in circulation (including funds stored in banks) as 'inalienable personal hoards'. Against his hoard, called 'money on the street', an individual man 'makes' his future (*fazer futuro*) through constant movement, creating further recombinations of relationships (Fotta 2019). Each such hoard is a multiple object, a "vague whole" (Verran 2007: 181) that, through the constant circulation of information and gossip within a community, remains virtually visible and encompassed by a specific morality.

Like 'classic' hoards, money on the street is not alienated but instead serves as a source of others' trust (Peebles 2014: 606). It is also "immobile" (Peebles 2008: 240), although this immobility takes on a specific form: whether in circulation or in a bank, as a source of one's particular value, money on the street is stored primarily with Jurons, partly outside the community. My argument proceeds as follows. First, as a meshwork of dyadic exchanges, money on the street co-creates and maintains a man's physical and social place in the world. Second, as an aggregate of sums payable in the future by both Jurons and Calon, money on the street is premised on a man's actions. Third, as an inalienable, singularized quantity, it is a source of stability that allows myriad exchanges to circulate around it. Fourth, as a concrete amount, it turns transactions into events whereby concrete sums detached from it express people's relationships. Thus, we can describe this entity as a hoard, treating it not only as value storage but also as a multiple object. Its qualities complicate the "colonization" (nationalization) (Peebles 2008: 238) of Calon futures by the state, which is predicated upon the radical, definitive financial inclusion of the population, even though, counter-intuitively, Calon use numbers to speak about relationships and to participate in the current credit economy. In this way, as shown next, they manage to uphold their individual agency as well as the autonomy of their communal life.

## Singularized Totalities

After his death, people talked approvingly about Vaqueiro as somebody who "always returned home with full bags," adding that "meat was never lacking" in his household. When a man marries, he starts living in a house or tent that is furnished by the bride's family and becomes responsible for providing for his household. He lends 'his' and 'his wife's' money—the dowry—to other Calon, but especially to Jurons. This capacity to generate circulatory velocity is sometimes glossed over as 'making' the future. The ultimate aim is to establish (*estabelecer*) or stabilize oneself. Success in doing so would be typically narrated thus: "I came here with X reals in my pocket, and then I established myself."

This capacity is a key aspect of a man's *força*: a level of potency and the power to impose, through demonstrations of manhood, the signs of this potency (Fotta 2016a). Settlements emerge around men with great *força*, and for Calon a good life means living *apoiado*, that is, in a supported manner (see also Ferrari 2010). Interlocking relationships become materialized in the arrangement of tents: children dwell beside their parents, and the strongman's dwelling is normally the largest, while the space before it serves as a central plaza where gossip and money circulate. A man's *força* is made visible in the positioning of his tent and in being surrounded by members of his family who will stand up for him. It is also realized in egalitarian, agonistic deals or card games with other Calon, or in one's reputation among Jurons. Money is crucial: a respected man does not become a strongman if he happens to be poor, while a rich man who refuses to meet people's expectations is without shame. The weddings of a man's children, which provide opportunities to host other Calon, are the main proof of his efficacy and establishment. News that circulates about weddings talks about their sumptuousness and about the amounts of dowry money, which are sometimes announced publicly at the ceremonies.

In exchanges that are realized or planned, as well as in discussions about them, money inscribes the space of one's potency. Small day-to-day loans between those living together characterize settlement life. Deferred (and renegotiable) payments among equals within people's home ranges create moments within which manhood can be forged. Individual exchanges, however, do not enact one's reputation independently, and having a reputation for keeping one's word and paying one's debts is not enough. Rather, a man is lent specific sums against his money on the street, a set of his exchanges—their quality as well as quantity—and the creditability that it implies. If a man is talked about as *morto* or *mulon*—'dead' in Portuguese and in Romany, respectively—he is not expected to make much money in the future, and his borrowing capacity will be constrained. Yet a man who was without any cash and had to sell his refrigerator for R$250 to buy groceries had, just a few weeks earlier, been lent R$10,000 to gamble with other Calon. He lost the entire sum. It was explained to me that this man was young and a *ganhador*: he had several bigger deals on the street that, in a few years time, would bring in cash. His wife also came from a strong family. All of this represents a form of hysteresis (see introduction, this volume). How people—men and women[3]—evaluate transactions between two

Calon men does not depend solely on the history of their acts, but also on their current state—including familial situation and relationships between parties in exchanges—and what the velocity of their money suggests about the future.

The process of maintaining one's environment and social standing by means of individual exchanges and of an aggregate object that emerges as a condensation of these transactions ends at death. A man's death is treated as unimaginable or astonishing, even if it follows a period of illness (Vilar 2011: 39–40). Death is accompanied by de-objectification of the man's attributes and the space his presence conjured. His tent is destroyed, and the surrounding settlement—the objectification of his unique assemblage of relationships—is abandoned. His death destabilizes people's life-worlds. Households from his settlement disperse across the region, some forming new groups, others joining relatives elsewhere. This alters relationships within settlements across the area.

A man's death also influences others' capacities to meet their obligations and requires adjustments to their plans. When Vaqueiro died, the total of his debts to other Calon was higher than that of the money owed to him, either by Calon or by Jurons. While Jair inherited debts owed to Vaqueiro, Vaqueiro's debts to Calon were forgotten.[4] The first multitude co-created Vaqueiro's singularized totality, his money on the street, and was premised on enchaining others' behavior, either as honorable Calon or as Juron clients under contract. Jair assumed these debts and Vaqueiro's clients. The second set—all future payments Vaqueiro owed—can be imagined as forming parts of many sets pertaining to many men. After his death, however, there was nobody whose behavior would be enchained by these specific sums. Jair spoke of this money as *dissimulado* (concealed, hidden). Vaqueiro's debts could no longer be considered part of creditors' money on the street, forcing them and their wider community to change their plans, especially if the debts were large.

Sons of a deceased man (or other heirs) do not inherit his debts to others or the reputation tied up with his deals. But they do acquire debts owed to him, relying on the moral behavior of the living. As with dowry money, others always have some idea of sums inherited. Each man's place in the world then depends upon, and is fabricated through, his deal making. Clearly, being the son of a well-established man and marrying a woman with a large dowry are advantageous. Through moneylending, a man makes his living and creates his own web of relations. He must be skilled in seizing chances and evaluating others, but nobody is blamed for not lending a large sum to a poor or untrustworthy person, even a relative. Through moneylending, a man earns his living and reputation, which become aspects of his strength.[5]

However, his unique web of dyadic relations are not simply triadic, presupposing witnesses (Munn 1992: 115), but complexly multiple, since Calon are aware that the existence of deals and their character—size, velocity, and so on—influence many others at various scales. Many deals are made in front of other Calon, and specific Jurons are known as clients of particular Calon. Above all, money on the street is thought of as potentially visible. Although it is virtual, as a temporary whole composed of money in loans, money on the street is more stable than specific transactions that a man counts upon. In its ability to index individual deals to itself, the hoard casts a net over a man's sphere of influence, anchoring his life.

## Temporary Wholes

Individual loans are guided by standardized local numeric logarithms that unite valuation with relations between actors and time, which are logarithmic relations themselves. For instance, a Calon lends R$30,000 for R$50,000 to be paid, say, on Christmas day in two years to another local Calon, but lends R$300 for R$500 to be paid by a Juron in 30 days. The logic of loans to Calon differs from those to Jurons. If a borrower cannot pay on time, the loan is renegotiated anew as a separate event when a Calon is concerned, while for Juron, interest payments are fixed and (normally) each month this sum is automatically claimed (cf. Schmidt, this volume). This is achieved by demanding that debtors pay the interest while keeping the principal. Collateral is never demanded from a Calon, although a welfare benefit might be 'sold' for cash for a certain period, and promissory notes can be used for deals among more distant individuals. Each Calon man has several loans to different people at any given moment that are repayable at different dates. In moneylenders' houses (whether Cigano or not), loans become objectified as piles of collateral objects, such as jewelry or car keys but especially predated checks, promissory notes, or bank and social benefit cards with pin numbers.[6] 'Weak' men have few of these artifacts and often carry them in their wallets. In both cases, they remain hidden from the view of others.

Much talk in Calon settlements revolves around who borrowed from whom, who paid whom, who lost in a card game, and so on. Keeping track of individuals' deals helps with assessing their reliability and with updating arrangements according to changed circumstances. For instance, a young man might imagine a future absolute sum two steps ahead. After receiving R$3,000 from a Juron in two months, he plans to persuade a rich Calon to borrow the whole sum for two years for R$7,000. At any moment, his money on the street thus composes a temporary whole. At the first moment $(t_0)$, this money $M(t_0)$ looks to him as $loan_1$, $loan_2 \rightarrow 3,000$. Two months later $(t_0 + 2)$, all other loans remaining equal but with their repayment closer, possibly even imminent, $M(t_0 + 2)$ appears as $loan_1$, $loan_2 \rightarrow 7,000$. But it is not only the absolute, quantitative sum, but also the relative quality of money on the street that has changed. The young man's negotiating position within the community becomes different when he can use the sum owed to him by the rich Calon as an argument for his liquidity.[7]

While particular loans are repayable at different moments, money on the street is always talked about as a summation, bringing the future into the present. In this process, two 'wholes' are produced simultaneously: a man's money on the street (a set of all debts owed to him) and the community of Calon who relate to this whole (a set of all Calon who discuss this hoard and its size). Creditworthiness takes into account assessments of another's hoard, but this whole is imprecise, unstable, and changes in character along with changed attributes of persons. Young and recently married men are known to have specific sums in circulation, the bulk of which originates in their wives' dowries. Their larger loans are usually made to Calon who are deemed more reliable,[8] which makes these deals more public. Established strongmen have long-term Juron clients involved in larger deals and are also known to have money in bank accounts. Their wholes are less visible and can only be deduced and suspected. Being considered 'rich', 'strong', 'established', 'young', 'poor', 'weak', or 'dead' is accompanied by specific assessments of how much money a man has on the street, as well as the quality of his loans. For other Calon, one's hoard is a 'vague whole'. For instance, Calon in São Gabriel were talking about a man in a distant town who could afford three lawyers to defend his son. This man, who was apparently worth R\$3,000,000, spent R\$100,000. In reality, there was only one lawyer, and the other two numbers are probably not exact either. At the same time, men make sure that others learn a version of their worth. After a failed attempt to marry off his son, a man exclaimed that his son did not need this bride's dowry since he (the father) had "300,000 on the street." In the company of others, men often recount various sums they are owed and by whom. Such rumors shape how men are perceived by potential partners.

Although loans are repayable on different dates, following different temporalities and logics of repayment, they are still a man's money *na rua* (on the street), *em giro* (in circulation), or, rarely, *no banco* (in a bank). This does not include a man's debts, although these play a role in evaluating his ability to meet obligations. The singularized totality of a man's money on the street stands for money he can count on if he collected all his loans, a capacity that is not guaranteed. Not only do one's debtors die or move away, but in order to remain in towns where he is successful, a man must sometimes accept defaults. Nevertheless, rather than the particular exchanges of which it is composed, it is money on the street as a whole that, partly through its intrinsic indeterminacy and instability, becomes a source of stability and co-creates a specific environment within which a man's actions find meaning.

## Performing Caloninity

A rich Calon man who refuses to 'liberate money' (*soltar dinheiro*) and provide his daughter with a sufficient dowry is deemed shamelessly calculating. I have argued elsewhere (Fotta 2016a) that strength and shame constitute two key Calon values realized as attributes of social persons (see also Ferrari 2010). What interests me here is that people who pass judgments about the appropriateness and character of a sum that was spent, withheld, or otherwise changed hands hold some notion of the total amount of money a man has on the street, and this becomes a ground against which the precise figure involved appears. Neither a man's money on the street nor the sum or the relationship between such figures is the exact representation of facts. These numbers are not "performances of the truth" but "truthful performances" (Ferrari 2010: 183). Like the money reportedly spent attempting to save Vaqueiro, these monies produce effects in the world as they communicate relationships between people (ibid.: 182). It is no accident that sums are exact quantities of money. Numerical quantification enacts non-calculability and unaccountability involved in the moment of expenditure. It signals people's commitment to Calon ethics and their moral discontinuity with Jurons, as well as openness to having their actions submitted to the questioning and assessment of others.

To appreciate how individual expenditures realize ethical commitment through 'mathematizing' difference from Jurons as the ontological premise of Caloninity, it is useful to approach money on the street as a multiple object. As Holbraad (2005) argues, money's quantitative quality does not necessarily turn money into a catalyst of calculation and abstraction. He shows that within Cuban Ifá divination, moments of expenditure foreground exact quantities of money spent while simultaneously highlighting the encompassment of one's money by divine injunction. Money serves as an appropriate medium for religious practices because a specific sum spent obviates calculation and commensuration between domains. It precludes other possible expenditures. While leaving a 'dent' in the totality of money possessed (or yet to be earned), the sum performs the ultimate divine encompassment of the totality itself. The expended sum allows that the divine claim to the sum could have been made in the first place. Crucially, in divination, money is not assigned to religious purposes and is not separated from money used in non-religious arenas (as, say, in the Christian tithe). Rather than connecting a transient individual life to a transcendent order in this manner, individual exchanges in Ifá practices, Holbraad maintains, "*fuse* everyday with the divine" (ibid.: 250n14; emphasis in original).

Similarly, the maintenance of Caloninity via money is not premised on a rejection of the abstracting potential of modern money, for instance, through earmarking some money[9] or by treating some transactions as linked to a societal core. Rather, all transactions (even those imagined to take place in the future) circle around one's money on the street, which they co-constitute as a life-world specific to each man.[10] For this reason, moments of sums' displacements can become sites of the 'metonymic' (cf. Gay y Blasco 2011) reproduction of Caloninity as a materialization of Calon values through the actions and comportment of gendered social persons. Expenditures 'fuse' scrutiny of their appropriateness and meaning with the reconstitution of Calon society through the circulation of knowledge about sums and by enchaining others in future obligations.

Morally evaluated expenditures—with most exchanges being deemed worthy of discussion to assess their meaning—highlight the encompassment of money on the street by ethical injunction. As they foreground refusal to calculate, transactions as events limit abstraction from social relationships by the calculative reasoning that social scientific common sense would predict for social life that relies on talking about relationships and behavior in terms of monetary values. Only when one lives alone or is considered *mulon* (dead), that is, when one is without credit or money on the street recognized as an inalienable hoard, can one avoid inviting others' scrutiny of one's strength. Being socially dead comes with submission to other socio-temporal regimes, such as those promoted by financial institutions or by Jurons more broadly.

As a multitude of exchanges with different partners—and simultaneously as a temporary whole—money on the street becomes the ground against which one's acts and relationships with others are made to appear as figures. When people talk about sums lost at cards, spent on a daughter's wedding, or involved in a deal with another Calon, they do so with the knowledge, however imperfect, of the quality of quantity of a man's money on the street. Exact sums make relationships visible by being related to this whole. Indeed, for most events, especially emergencies, men must borrow money against their money in circulation or against money that others expect them to make in the future. While money might be actually, or potentially, made through predatory loans to Jurons and seen as a resource to be constantly reinvested, money on the street exists as a hoard only thanks to its modal encompassment in Calon values (see Fotta 2016a: 209). In this sense, money on the street is "already spent" (Olivera 2016: 156). Because particular transactions indexically relate the sums to his whole and hence to his community, they become events in which a man recreates himself as a Calon.

## The Hoards of Bankers of the Hinterland

Anthony Pickles (2013: 515) argues that Gorokans in Papua New Guinea "know that pockets hide, but they imagine their insides contain money." This quality of pockets makes them an appropriate tool for concealing money and for making relations visible whenever sums leave them. In some ways, 'the street' among Calon serves the same purpose. When a sum indexed to a man's money on the street is used in a way that actualizes a specific relationship with another, and hence with all other Calon as witnesses, it permits evaluation of his behavior. But unlike pockets, the street is not so much imagined as containing money. Rather, people are 'known' or 'said' to have specific sums in circulation. The point is not that these individual hoards are truly invisible or opaque (Peebles 2014: 604) and therefore sources of hidden power (see also Graeber 1996), but that they are pictured as ultimately transparent and therefore the objects of their owners' creativity and others' claims.

If Bahians think of Calon as 'bankers', they are not completely incorrect. This is not only because Ciganos lend money, but also because Calon remain 'unbanked'. Peebles (2008, 2014) argues that in the nineteenth century banks alienated people's money by turning it into savings and credit, but that they did not alienate this money further, instead keeping it as reserves. Calon, even when they put some money in banks and circulate it in loans, treat them as co-composing their monies on the street, as their inalienable hoards. The power of these hoards, which enable the creation and maintenance of a unique mode of life, lies within the Calon community, while individuals' projects for their futures are not alienated to formal institutions. Thus, Calon 'unbanking' is an aspect of cosmological self-determination in its own right (Peebles 2014).

This situation is historically specific. Calon's occupation as moneylenders is tied to the financialization and monetization of daily life in Bahia, while their preoccupation with money on the street might suggest a struggle over the character of money, debts, and communities. This preoccupation is linked to the practice of moneylending and its dangers. Today, more so than in the past, Calon can make money individually and hide it in banks and among Jurons, which might be seen as threatening proper Calon sociability. Yet Calon have used these new alignments to recreate themselves anew as Ciganos. For Calon Gypsies, money's character of multiplicity is tied to the creation of Calon community as a unique mode of being in the world. By composing their own money on the street, individual men fabricate their own place in the world, within which a "commonality" of ethos (Gay y Blasco 2001: 642) finds its expression. By creatively exploiting the affordances of money on the street's quantity, Calon men create their network of exchange partners and their reputation for financial acumen at the same time as they fabricate the very basis against which their performances are actualized.

## Acknowledgments

I am grateful to Ville Koskinen, Sandy Ross, and especially Mario Schmidt for their observations and suggestions on various drafts of this chapter, which forced me to rethink its arguments and conclusions substantially. The research for this chapter was partially supported by the Wenner-Gren Foundation and the German Research Foundation (DFG; grant FO 983/1-1).

---

**Martin Fotta** is a Postdoctoral Research Fellow at the Institut für Ethnologie, Goethe-Universität Frankfurt am Main. He is currently working on a research project about the effects of conditional cash transfers on the indebtedness of rural households in Brazil. His publications include *From Itinerant Trade to Moneylending in the Era of Financial Inclusion* (2018) and, with co-editor Maria Elisa Balen, *Money from the Government in Latin America: Conditional Cash Transfer Programs and Rural Lives* (2019).

## Notes

1. A Hungarian inter-war currency, pengö is legendary for having suffered the most serious hyperinflation ever recorded.
2. Unless otherwise indicated, all translations are my own.
3. While women are normally not directly involved in moneylending, their role in influencing their husbands and in circulating information is crucial for the functioning of this system.
4. Calon avoid borrowing cash from Jurons and are highly critical of those who do so.
5. A man's reputation is sometimes referred to as *crédito* (credit) or *nome* (name).
6. Calon 'sell' their welfare benefit cards to one another for cash for specified periods rather than pawn them, as is the case with Jurons.
7. These 'wholes' are 'multiple multiples'. While the young man knew how much he had on the street, and others guessed or learned a sum, both sets were related to how much he and others assumed the rich man had, and so on.
8. Weak (*fraco*) men also prefer to lend to Calon. They are seen as 'afraid' to make deals with Jurons.
9. Such dynamics might play a role when, for instance, a man makes a point of stressing that in a particular transaction he is investing his wife's money that his son will inherit when he is mature. In this manner, the man is already composing his son's money on the street, helping to bring about the latter's singular place in the world while recreating his own.
10. The moves are related. A man can be considered honorable for providing his daughter with a sizable dowry, but because the amount he is believed to have in circulation changes as a result, further lending to him can be considered a liability.

## References

Billi, Marcelo. 2005. "No Sertão da Bahia, Cigano é 'Banqueiro.'" *Folha de São Paulo*, 12 June.

Brazzabeni, Micol, Manuela I. Cunha, and Martin Fotta, eds. 2016. *Gypsy Economy: Romani Livelihoods and Notions of Worth in the 21st Century.* New York: Berghahn Books.

Day, Sophie, Celia Lury, and Nina Wakeford. 2014. "Number Ecologies: Numbers and Numbering Practices." *Distinktion* 15 (2): 123–154.

Day, Sophie, Evthymios Papataxiarchis, and Michael Stewart, eds. 1998. *Lilies of the Field: Marginal People Who Live for the Moment.* Boulder, CO: Westview Press.

Ferrari, Florencia. 2010. "O Mundo Passa: Uma Etnografia dos Calon e Suas Relações com os Brasileiros." PhD diss., Universidade de São Paulo.

Fotta, Martin. 2016a. "Exchange, Shame and Strength among the Calon of Bahia: A Values-Based Analysis." In Brazzabeni et al. 2016, 201–220.

Fotta, Martin. 2016b. "Householding against Work." Unpublished.

Fotta, Martin. 2019. "'Only the Dead Don't Make the Future': Calon Lives between Non-Gypsies and Death." *Journal of the Royal Anthropological Institute* 25 (3): 587–605.

Gay y Blasco, Paloma. 2001. "'We Don't Know Our Descent': How the Gitanos of Jarana Manage the Past." *Journal of Royal Anthropological Institute* 7 (4): 631–647.

Gay y Blasco, Paloma. 2011. "Agata's Story: Singular Lives and the Reach of the 'Gitano Law.'" *Journal of the Royal Anthropological Institute* 17 (3): 445–461.

Gilbert, Emily. 2005. "Common Cents: Situating Money in Time and Place." *Economy and Society* 34 (3): 357–388.

Graeber, David. 1996. "Beads and Money: Notes toward a Theory of Wealth and Power." *American Ethnologist* 23 (1): 4–24.

Holbraad, Martin. 2005. "Expending Multiplicity: Money in Cuban Ifá Cults." *Journal of the Royal Anthropological Institute* 11 (2): 231–254.

Manrique, Nathalie. 2016. "'Give and Don't Keep Anything!' Wealth, Hierarchy and Identity among the Gypsies of Two Small Towns in Andalusia, Spain." In Brazzabeni et al. 2016, 221–239.

Meillassoux, Quentin. 2008. *After Finitude: An Essay on the Necessity of Contingency.* Trans. Ray Brassier. New York: Continuum.

Müller, Lúcia. 2014. "Negotiating Debts and Gifts: Financialization Policies and the Economic Experiences of Low-Income Social Groups in Brazil." *Vibrant: Virtual Brazilian Anthropology* 11 (1): 191–221.

Munn, Nancy D. 1992. *The Fame of Gawa: A Symbolic Study of Value of Transformation in a Massim (Papua New Guinea) Society.* Durham, NC: Duke University Press.

Olivera, Martin. 2016. "The Mechanism of Independence: Economic Ethics and Domestic Mode of Production among Gabori Roma." In Brazzabeni et al. 2016, 145–162.

Peebles, Gustav. 2008. "Inverting the Panopticon: Money and the Nationalization of the Future." *Public Culture* 20 (2): 233–265.

Peebles, Gustav. 2014. "Rehabilitating the Hoard: The Social Dynamics of Unbanking in Africa and Beyond." *Africa* 84 (4): 595–613.

Pickles, Anthony J. 2013. "Pocket Calculator: A Humdrum 'Obviator' in Papua New Guinea?" *Journal of the Royal Anthropological Institute* 19 (3): 510–526.

Stewart, Michael. 1994. "La Passion pour l'argent: Les forints, i rup et l'ambiguité de l'argent chez les Tsiganes Hongrois." *Terrain* 23: 45–62.

Stewart, Michael. 1997. *The Time of the Gypsies.* Boulder, CO: Westview Press.

Thiele, Maria E. 2008. "Geschichte und Mystifizierung der Zigeuner in Brasilien." In *Roma-/Zigeunerkulturen in neuen Perspektiven: Romani/Gypsy Cultures in New Perspectives*, ed. Johannes Ries and Fabian Jacobs, 135–154. Leipzig: Leipziger Universitätsverlag.

Verran, Helen. 2007. "The Telling Challenge of Africa's Economies." *African Studies Review* 50 (2): 163–182.

Vilar, Márcio. 2011. "Vom Dreißigsten Tag nach dem Tod eines alten Calon in Brasilien." In *Vielheiten: Leipziger Studien zu Roma/Zigeuner-Kulturen*, ed. Theresa Jacobs and Fabian Jacobs, 35–49. Leipzig: Leipziger Universitätsverlag.

Vilar, Márcio. 2016. "'A Vida do Cigano: Trauerrituale, Person und Tauschkreisläufe bei Calon-Zigeunern im Nordosten Brasiliens." PhD diss. University of Leipzig.

Williams, Patrick. 1982. "The Invisibility of the Kalderash of Paris: Some Aspects of the Economic Activity and Settlement Patterns of the Kalderash Rom of the Paris Suburbs." *Urban Anthropology* 11 (3–4): 315–346.

Williams, Patrick. 2003. *Gypsy World: The Silence of the Living and the Voices of the Dead.* Trans. Catherine Tihanye. Chicago: University of Chicago Press.

*Chapter 7*

# WHAT IS MONEY?
## A Definition beyond Materiality and Quantity

*Emanuel Seitz*

This chapter takes seriously this edited volume's claim that money's quantity is material. Three questions, however, arise at once. First, what is money? Second, is quantity an essential property of money? Third, is materiality an essential property of money? An adequate response to the last two questions depends on the answer to the first one. To answer it, this chapter presents, in the spirit of dialectic education, some basic properties of money by using (but not writing) the history of monetary theory. Dialectical writing in the Aristotelian sense implies a certain style that is uncommon among contemporary scholarly articles. First, I refer to well-known scientific approaches that try to determine the relations between mathematics and money in order to discuss their merits and demerits. Keynes was chosen because he exemplifies an economist's view, Spengler for his historical approach, which exhibits striking similarities with sociological and anthropological perspectives on money. Spengler's cultural relativism and his strict reduction of thinking patterns—that is, 'modes of thought'—to external influences, such as environment, civilization, or culture, provide useful notions to think with and reflect upon.

The method of ancient dialectics (Wagner and Rapp 2004: 14–15) further requires that one follows the dialogue partners—in this case, authors—within the logic of their arguments until reaching a point of inconsistency or puzzlement. Therefore, my goal is not to judge the texts on the rightness or wrongness of their premises, but to look for critical points where the structure of their arguments and their concepts must be redefined. This method aims to avoid falling prey to prejudices and to clarify underlying assumptions. Impatient readers may criticize this writing method as meandering, perhaps resembling a drunken hobo, unable to defend any clear-cut thesis. However, my aim is to sharpen and define conceptualizations of money's quantity and materiality through juxtaposition and dialogue between well-known authors. This method enables me to recognize the place of money within the whole of these thinkers' epistemic systems. By thus understanding former reflections on money as potentially still valid contributions to contemporary monetary theory, I will use Plato's and Aristotle's reflections on money to conclude with a conception of money that is strictly opposed to a position that reduces the science of money to mere mathematical knowledge. This does not mean that my conception gets rid of numbers and arithmetical operations; on the contrary, these notions remain attached to the concept of money.

Why are money's materialities and quantities problematic? The amount of book money—digital money and payment obligations—is much higher than the amount of cash. In January 2015, for example, the amount of cash was one-tenth of the countable monetary aggregates in the euro area (European Central Bank 2015). Thus, there is a gap between materialized forms of money and money's quantity. One could say that there is both more and less money than exists. For orthodox economists, the abstract amounts of money refer to actual objects serving as money. Contrarily, several sociological conceptualizations of money, based on Marx ([1867] 2007: 49–99) and Simmel ([1900] 2004: 259–283), posit that abstract quantity is the main quality of money. These theories assume that monetary quantification automatically has alienating and modernizing effects on a society as a whole (cf. Paul 2012) and that these abstract numbers refer to fictitious forms of money unsupported by assets. By identifying money with debt, and thereby dematerialized money, Graeber (2011) suggests that this question is meaningless because money is, first and foremost, a debt upheld and structured by violent power mechanisms. By calling debt a "promise corrupted by both math and violence" (ibid.: 391) and reducing money to a power mechanism, Graeber's account tries to avoid the problem of how money's quantity and materiality are connected.

The position that argues that 'money-is-a-thing' can be called materialistic; the position that argues that monetary objects are representatives of value can be loosely called immaterialist. From a logical point of view, there are only four possibilities. First, materialist views are true, and the immaterialist is wrong. Second, materialist views are wrong, and the immaterialist is true. Third, both are true, but insufficient. Fourth, both are wrong, the position of

Graeber. It seems quite obvious that money has at least something to do with material monetary objects and immaterial quantitative abstractness; therefore, the fourth possibility is excluded. I will argue for the third possibility, seeking a third property that is essential, while understanding quantity and materiality as contingent properties of money.

My dialogical argument evolves in three stages. First, a close reading of Spengler offers an immaterial definition of money as a human mental concept or mode of thought and not an object with specific functions used for specific purposes. The shortcomings of Spengler's theory led me to Plato and Aristotle in the second stage. In their view, monetary functions are not derived from objects in specific situations, like exchange, but from humans and their needs in these specific contexts. Thus, money's purposes are extrinsic; there is no other nature of money than the ends that it facilitates. I then move to Keynes's classification of money according to its properties of quantity and materiality.

I will thereby present a discussion on the ontology of money while aiming to avoid oversimplification or overcomplication. A short discussion of two recent works on money might be illuminating here. Firstly, Noam Yuran (2014: 7) suggests that money is desire, but he admits that his argument "grounds money in desire without committing itself to a precise conception of desire." Such a replacement of a word under scrutiny with another word that remains undefined is clearly not helpful and just postpones the problem; it is an example of oversimplification. Secondly, Nigel Dodd (2014: 4) aims to address "all of [money's] myriad complexity," which he calls the "social life of money" (ibid.: 5). His conceptualization of money as an idea is a quite promising ontological claim, but the enumeration of items and topics and the specific situations connected to the object of investigation cannot illuminate the totality of an idea or determine what anything is. Dodd's narration offers much and useful information about former thoughts and discussions on money in a remarkably readable form, but less knowledge about what is essential and what is accidental. This indifference prevents an answer to the question of what money is by overcomplicating the question.

## Spengler: Money as Abstract Immateriality

Oswald Spengler's ([1923] 1963) *Der Untergang des Abendlandes* (*The Decline of the West*) is among the few works that describe the relationship between money, its materiality, and its multiplicity. Spengler defines money in contrast to current theories as follows (ibid.: 1163):

> Es ist ein Fehler aller modernen Geldtheorien, dass sie vom Wertzeichen oder sogar vom Stoff der Zahlungsmittel statt von der Form des wirtschaftlichen Denkens ausgehen. Aber Geld ist wie Zahl und Recht *eine Kategorie des Denkens*.

> It is an error of all modern money-theories that they start from the value-token or even the material of the payment-medium instead of from the form of economic thought. In reality, money, like number and law, is a category of thought.[1]

To understand the phrase 'category of thought', it is necessary to view it in light of Spengler's conceptual framework. Although defending cultural relativism, Spengler ([1923] 1963: 234–280) classifies different types of mathematics and monies, analogous to stages of civilization, as "magic," "Apollinian," and "Faustian." These categorizations represent three distinct, characteristic ways to reflect on money and its relationship to mathematics and materiality, regardless of their historical veracity. For Spengler, money as a category of thought is, in its wider sense, any imagined configuration between money as an object (its materiality) and money as a non-object (its quantity). Thus, money is not just a tool to pay. In a narrower sense, real monetary thought requires what Marx ([1867] 2007: 79) has called a "general form of value" that depends on a cognitive and uniform calculation system of value and, in its final form, on an object in which it materializes itself.

The magic mode of thinking, however, operates without abstraction and without mathematics. A distinctive feature of these magic, or Magian, cultures—synonymous with those called 'primitive' or 'pre-modern' in classical anthropology—is "to compare goods" and not to "reckon values" (Spengler 1926: 2:482). Instead of calculating, counting, and accounting prices, magic cultures make estimations, based on comparisons that Grimm appropriately named 'poetic' (cf. Echterhölter, this volume). For magic cultures, quantity cannot be detached from quality and the media of exchange are not representations of an abstract amount of countable value. For Spengler, magic cultures are examples of civilizations with no money in a narrow sense, either as object or as non-object, because they lack a general form of value as a category of thought.

Spengler's second mode, Apollinian, corresponds to classical antiquity and the Renaissance; it entails abstraction linked to magnitude, but not to function (as in Faustian, modern thought). A characteristic of Apollinian economics is a lack of abstractions that are completely detached from the physical world. Within these cultures, wealth, capital, income, and debt are conceived not as economic potential but as the sum of valuables that someone wears or keeps in a treasure chamber.

> Antiker Reichtum ist kein Guthaben, sondern ein Geldhaufen. (Spengler [1923] 1963: 1171)

> Classical Wealth does not consist in a bank balance, but in piling money.[2]

In Spengler's framework, Apollinian credit is only a shift of money recompensed with a charge that would now be called an interest rate. For lenders, money is gone for a certain time span; for debtors, money borrowed becomes part of their current wealth and property, although it must be returned. Modern money creation by fractional reserve banking was thus impossible in such cultures, because lending money that was already loaned could not be categorically conceived (Spengler 1926: 2:469–496). The Apollinian monetary mode of thought is limited to money as an object. Money as a non-object can only be imagined as an amount of money currently residing at another place or in another physical form, but not as pre-existing the actualization of that amount.

Money that one potentially possesses in the future is thus not credit fabricated *ex nihilo*, but rather part of a money chain made of solid, already existing gold that could potentially be used as money. Oakley (this volume) describes this potential form of cash—this monetary object that is not money-proper—as para-money. The difference between the Apollinian mode of thought and modern conceptions of money can be detected in the hoarding practice of Calon Gypsies (cf. Fotta, this volume). Calon men use an Apollinian way of hoarding in a Faustian monetary system. They appear to be using money in a way that maximizes its 'potential', as is expected in a Faustian culture. Yet in Fotta's analysis, the purpose of hoarded money is not maximized potential, but wealth in another form that sits 'ready to use'. The bank cards that the Calon money-lenders keep, like the Tudor money chains Oakley (this volume) describes, constitute money that is ready to be converted into another form, not abstracted potential. At first sight, their conception of wealth seems similar, but in fact Calon also hoard in the modern way, through a bank balance, and represent their wealth with one number indicating monetary potential.

According to Spengler ([1923] 1963: 71–124), the Apollinian mode of thought relies upon a form of mathematics operating with numbers and quantities as magnitude and proportion, while modern, Faustian mathematics uses functions, potential, and symbolic expressions. Thus, Faustian money permits thinking about money as a non-object. From Adam Smith's *Wealth of Nations* ([1776] 2007: 496–520) onward, theoretical approaches to money avoid identifying wealth with cash by introducing meta-categories bound to symbolic and function-like expressions of wealth (cf. Simiand [1934] 2006: 218–227). Smith's ([1776] 2007: 4) understanding of "the annual labour of every nation" as a "fund" would have been incomprehensible within a thing-based, Magian, or Apollinian theory of money. Smith's thinking develops within a mathematical framework that calculates wealth with the function, $f(x)$, with $x$ defined as labor. The definition of money as a medium serving three or four monetary functions (Jevons 1896: 13–18), which, as a general outline, is also supported by modern anthropologists (Hart 2012: 147–159), could also be considered an example that supports Spengler's theory. As a central paradigm shift, the definition of money as a function does not mean that three or four tasks of monetary objects are merely described, but that a formula is developed that allows identifying any object as money if the specific conditions are met.

As a consequence, accounts of the primitive origins of money can be classified as a kind of *petitio principii* insofar as a scholar fixes in advance either what monetary objects are or what monetary functions are. Thus, in tracing the historical origins of money, analysts find sets of perishable goods, ornaments, or prestige items that were later transformed into money or gave a monetary unit its name (cf. Einzig 1951; Gerloff 1952; Laum 1924). However, as soon as these objects are defined as money, the set of monetary functions needs to be expanded. In contrast, some twentieth-century anthropologists and historians have spent much effort demonstrating that these objects are not money because they circulate in apparently non-market economies (cf. Bohannan 1955; Polanyi

1944; Sahlins 1972), and without markets the means of exchange cannot fulfill monetary functions properly. Analogously, contemporary approaches can be divided into analyses that are grounded in conceptions of money that are object-based or function-based (cf. Schmidt 2014, contra Heinsohn and Steiger 2002). Spengler's conceptualization of money as a mode of thought is an alternative to this dichotomy with its pseudo-empirical money origin myths. Yet in being tied to a pre-established definition, his historical analysis thereby 'suffers' from the same conceptual self-referentiality as any other historical analysis.

One way to escape this self-referentiality is to ask if Spengler's typology really describes modes of thought. For example, to relend already lent money is an action, not a thought. But Spengler is unable to see this because, in his view, modes of thought are not driven by humans, but rather drive humans. To summarize, one can reflect upon the immaterial character of money, but 'category of thought' remains a vague concept that circumscribes human actions rather than thoughts. If one wants to avoid the pitfalls of Spengler's theory, it is therefore necessary to think about human actions without reference to superstructures such as society or civilization as human-driving forces. Illuminating examples for such a mode of thought are the works of Plato and Aristotle.

## Money as a Connector of Exchange in Plato's *Republic*

In Plato's *Republic*, money is understood as something that must be discussed in relation to distributional actions and values. The dialogue partners, Glaukon, Adeimantos, and Socrates, debate about justice (*dikaiosyne*), not economy or the state. Socrates suggests imagining a state to explore justice on a bigger scale, but his goal is not a utopian model (Plato 2005: 368a). Rather, justice is closely related to suitable relations between need and distribution, within which money has its legitimation. Socrates' thought experiment starts with the development of the state according to basic human needs or *chreia*, which are defined as subsistence goods like food, clothes, and houses, as well as luxuries like pillows, perfumes, and prostitutes (Plato 2005: 368b–373d). In a perfect society, people's work provides these necessities; peasants, architects, servants, craftsmen, and many more professions are justified through the needs of others. Socrates thus assumes that people are not self-sufficient and that they therefore have (or want) to maintain contact with others. Just as merchants are introduced as actors distributing goods, money is described as a 'connector of exchange' (*symbolon tes allages*) that allows the distribution of goods inside a community whose relatively complex division of labor requires 'giving and counter-giving' (*metadidomi*) (ibid.: 371b). It remains ambiguous whether this connector is a thing, a word, or a promise.

Both *symbolon* and *metadidomi* are related to unspecified movements of something undetermined (a word, a thing) between undetermined people. These vague descriptions can resolve some tensions or puzzles of modern monetary theories, potentially avoiding the mistaken supposition of causal relations. My deliberately open definition of *symbolon* and *metadidomi* stands in stark contrast to metaphorical understandings of money as a 'symbol' or 'pledge' in an exchange that move away from the etymological sense of these two words. For an epistemology that relies on the historical context of Ancient Greece, *symbolon* must be seen as a token standing for a contract between two parties. Friends demonstrated hospitality by breaking an object in halves, each keeping half as a *symbolon* of the friendship (cf. Graeber 2011: 298–302). *Symbola* are thus parts that represent a whole of equal ontological status, that is, a relationship (cf. introduction, this volume). Such interpretations are reflected in contemporary chartalist and semiotic definitions of money (Graeber 2011: 47–54, 298–302, 340).

It is therefore no surprise that several current historical accounts on the history of monetary theory trace the origins of modern reflections back to Plato and Aristotle (cf. Brodbeck 2012: 398–460). Socrates' companions indeed interpret *metadidomi* as 'buying and selling', but it remains possible without overinterpreting Plato's text to assume that, for Socrates, these purchasing operations are only one type of giving and counter-giving. Narrow interpretations of distribution as buying and selling have led classical and neo-classical economists to frame Plato as a forerunner of their own ideas; however, their accounts miss the point that Plato's and Aristotle's conception is a complete inversion of modern economic thought. Liberating Aristotle and Plato from economic appropriations allows for a redefinition of money, not as a function of objects, but as a set of functions for humans. While for Smith ([1776] 2007: 15), the division of labor is a "consequence of a certain propensity in human nature … to truck, barter, and exchange," for Plato's dialogue partners, a certain propensity within communities to truck, barter, and exchange is a consequence of labor division. Socrates and his friends understand justice as functionality: every social need generates corresponding institutions and practices. Contrarily, Smith invents a biological genealogy for social processes: human nature automatically gives rise to specific practices and institutions.

Following Socrates, *metadidomi* can be defined as exchange without any notion of barter, gain, or profit, as a pure distributive interrelation that enables peasants to exchange but not sell their products. Thus, the division of labor requires intermediaries such as markets and money. In a Socratic sense, function is different from—almost opposed to—the notion of neo-classical functional theories. An object does not exist because it has a certain function. Rather, it is because of some need, some required use, that an object, practice, or institution arises. This pseudo-causal interrelation, expressed by 'because of' (*heneka*), describes the ends to which money is used and not what money is. In other words, Plato's dialogue understands the economy as a sphere of prudence beyond scientific knowledge and gives an idea of justice in economy, but not of money itself (even though it has been determined what money is). Within this sphere of moral and political judgment, both quantitative and material aspects of money can be considered side by side, although they are not as relevant, in this perspective, as the purpose of money.

## Means and Ends: How to Use Money Well

The fact that Plato's vague description of money provokes conflicting inter-pretations and misunderstandings might be intentional. For both Plato and Aristotle, money's fundamental nature is 'ethical' or 'pragmatic'. But what do Plato and Aristotle mean by 'ethical'? First, money as an object is not stable enough to allow an elaboration of a corpus of epistemic knowledge that is for-malized in axioms, terms, and equations as in mathematically inspired modern neo-classical economy. Rules and educative examples for dealing with money, economics, and the state are easily imaginable, but there are no laws that lie in the object itself. While modern mathematical economics still refers to some idea of a quantifiable *mathesis universalis* combined with a strict behavioral model (Redman 2003: 27–29),[3] Plato and Aristotle consider money practices and teach dispositions of using and gaining money because money cannot be known by contemplating it outside of practices or by elaborating a set of 'natural' laws.

Second, Plato's and Aristotle's reflections on money are limited to state-ments about what money is as a means. Aristotle's classical treatments of money in the *Nikomachian Ethics* (2007: 1133a–1134b) and *Politics* (2012: 1257a–1258b) refer more to human interactions wherein money appears than to money's nature. The fifth book of the *Ethics* is about justice, comparable to the Platonic dialogue discussed above. Distributional justice as a 'virtue' (*arete*) requires some kind of measurement, and money is the measure for 'needs' (*chreia*). The material qualities of money are driven by practical con-siderations; it remains unclear whether money as a good is the measurement instrument that is an object or a numéraire (counting unit) that is a mode of thought. Neither Plato's connector for exchange nor Aristotle's measure inter-pret money as a magnitude in a mathematical sense. Their accounts describe money according to how it functions when distribution is organized well. Thus, materiality and quantity are subordinated to the possibility of justice and using money well. With such an abstract definition of money, the question of quality or 'goodness' (of use) becomes more important than the material or numeral appearance (of money).

But what is meant by good quality or ethical goodness, especially in rela-tion to money? The 'good life' is the main topic of Hellenic ethics and provokes many misunderstandings relevant to money. As Heidegger ([1924] 2002: 80) argues, 'good' always has a double meaning for Aristotle: goodness as a qual-ity of an entity (essential), and goodness as a mode of being (existential). In the second sense, the goodness of money is a matter of how to realize the connection as a good one. Ethics in this sense is not just guidance on how to do something as a do-gooder, but also how to do something qualitatively well.

But how can the quantitative character of money as measure be related to such a notion of quality? The first possibility starts with a misleading equiva-lence. To locate the fundamentals of money in human action and ethics is not the same as to argue that money and economics are a matter of morality as if they would not be 'economical'. Several heterodox conceptions of economy regret the loss of virtues only in a moral sense and try to replace the problem of debt with guilt (cf. Graeber 2011; MacIntyre [1981] 2013; Sedláček 2012). As a consequence, money is reduced to subjective and somehow arbitrary judgments of individuals and groups about the best of values. The problem here is that moral goodness is only part of the goodness of actions, in addition to efficacy, beauty and so on. Neither a purely economical nor a purely moral conception of money goes far enough to grasp its character as a means of distributional actions (contra Holbraad, this volume).

The second way to think of the goodness of means, as followed by Plato and Aristotle, is to combine quality with quantity through money's purposes. But it is necessary to carefully examine how the argument of *telos* is employed, whether essential or existential. The essential approach is thinking in terms of reaching a distant goal. In that sense, money serves as a tool to acquire goods, and the goods are the goal of money. Such a treatment of money easily turns to the teleology of goals lying within money itself, as if money were not only the means but also the end of actions (Simmel [1900] 2009: 204–283, esp. 232–234). As a consequence, the use of money would create a propensity for bad habits like greed and avarice. From an existential perspective, like that of Plato and Aristotle, money gains its teleological character when the user sets a purpose. As a connector for exchange, money serves a diversity of potential purposes that connect through exchange, not for this or that specific purpose. Money as a means has an area of natural employment, but not a natural end. In the case of a knife, its area of employment is cutting, but its end can serve as well for murder as for cooking. In the case of money, its natural area of employment is exchange. One possible end could be distributional justice as a goal that is extrinsic to the essence of money. The expression 'connector for exchange' thereby remains deliberately undetermined.

When money is portrayed as a measure, its quantity becomes a precondition for measuring a qualitatively good (and just) distribution. Money does not measure because it is quantitative; money measures because humans need a measure and any measure is a qualified quantitative relation. Any supposed intrinsic quality of money's quantity to erode traditional communities can be disproved by cautious ethnographic examinations like those of Schmidt and Fotta (this volume). It seems more likely that certain habits of dealing with quantitative amounts of money and monetary objects can be artificially acquired as second nature, based on the principles of socially accepted or rejected practices (cf. Ross, this volume). Thus, it is not the quantitative character of money, but rather its connection to principles of actions that determines the goodness or badness of its effects. The nature of a means such as money is its purpose, and this purpose is realized through actions. Thus, the mode of action—money's mode of use—tells more about its intrinsic effects than its nature as a relation, which requires further determination of such relation's ends.

Users of money must develop competence while, and for, using it. The outcome of such practical training is prudence and cleverness as a form of knowledge (cf. Ross, this volume). Handling and manipulating money, not its being, was the main concern of Aristotle and Plato. Technical tricks for managing money are found in the second book of Aristotle's *Oikonomika* (2006). The other branch of teachable knowledge is advice on recognizing the correct ends of actions and how to perform and bring them to realization. Such practical guidance is addressed as *daimonia*, which could be bad (*kako-*) or good (*eu-*) (Arendt [1958] 1998: 192–207; Sloterdijk 2012: 253–298). One example of poor (although not necessarily morally wrong) conduct would be to earn money, which is a means, as an end in itself (Aristotle 2012: 1257a–1258b).

Aristotle would thus probably counter the classic statement 'money is what money does' with a simple question: "How can money do? It isn't animated. Men do" (cf. Arestis and Sawyer 2006: 139). The vague under-determination of money as a connector of exchange and a prerequisite for measuring thus originates in Plato's and Aristotle's conception of economics as a sphere of prudence and cleverness rather than epistemic knowledge. Thus, philosophy and ethics as a discipline of the good life can only give advice on how to act with money, because money is a means without intrinsic purpose. From this perspective, materiality and quantity become irrelevant properties in describing what money is. Plato's and Aristotle's practical description of money covers the multiplicity of historically attested forms of money only vaguely, but has three merits. First, it covers them all without becoming wrong. Second, the definition of money as a connector of exchange makes clear why the same objects were once interpreted as value tokens of gift exchange and later as forms of primitive money (Einzig 1951; Gerloff 1952; Laum 1924; contra Bohannan 1955; Polanyi 1944; Sahlins 1972). Gift economy and market economy are two forms of exchange, and the similar appearance of objects serving as exchange links has its origins in the notion of money itself as a connector.[4] Third, economists' multiple interpretations of *metadidomi, symbolon, allage* (exchange), and meter show the effectiveness of this ambiguity: it provokes opposition and resistance and promotes the motion of thought in scientific debates.

## What Is Money? Keynes's Diaeresis and the Rediscovery of Mathematics

Like Plato and Aristotle, John Maynard Keynes saw economics as a field of practical wisdom, and, in a rather Hellenic style of ethics, he hoped his *Treatise on Money* ([1930] 2011: vii) would be useful in conveying a "right understanding" of topics that are "of enormous practical importance to the well-being of the world." While Aristotle tried to define and promote just the well-being of individuals, states, or communities, Keynes takes over a modern, world perspective reserved for gods in antiquity. In contrast to Spengler, theoretical reflections and conceptual determination of a phenomenon are not sought for the sake of abstract knowledge about the world, but for practical purposes. Keynes ([1936] 2008) insists that his *General Theory of Employment, Interest and Money* is not a "scientific" theory in a strict sense of the word. Rather, it developed out of "an organised and orderly method of thinking out particular problems" (ibid.: 271), that is, a form of reasoning focused on problems that show up in practice (cf. Crespo 2013).

Keynes tries to determine connections between the material and quantitative aspects of money, or which 'side of the coin' is derived from the other. At first glance, it seems that Keynes does not pay much attention to two thousand years of discussion about money's functions, nature, and laws. Instead of examining the origin of money, he understands his historical reflections as illustrations for the 'classifications' he has made before without referring to historical examples. This inversion is not just a matter of style; it is also an index of a different mode of thought in contrast to neo-classical approaches, exemplified by Carl Menger's ([1909] 1970: 3–22, 92–97) essay on money, in which the origins of means of exchange are understood to precede and substantiate the definition of money. Keynes shows his modern readers how it is possible to avoid the epistemological problems of historicism that, as I have shown above, should have tantalized Spengler and some scholars interested in primitive monies. Historical evidence is not the source, but a reverse interpretation in accordance with current opinions that are considered true. Compared to Plato's and Aristotle's definitions of money, but also compared to his modern predecessors, Keynes's approach to integrating the material and quantitative parts of money is remarkably clear and distinct.

I believe this progress was made possible due to Keynes's extensive study of Aristotle's work and an adoption of his understanding of definitions (cf. Crespo 2014: 96–109; Dostaler 2007: 163–175). A *logos*, or philosophical discussion, must distinguish between concepts related to the topic, identifying which ones are the most important and setting aside irrelevant ones in order to develop a correct understanding. To achieve this, Keynes reanimated the ancient dialectical method of diaeresis: division into genus and species. While modern taxonomies represent the order of the world as being grounded in historical dependencies, diaeresis is a tool that creates clear, distinct definitions without reference to history. Having a clear concept of a house means knowing what a house is, while having a distinct concept is knowing its features and parts (Kant [1800] 2004: 527–587). The lack of logical hierarchy in modern functional definitions of money leads to a more or less clear, but indistinct, concept of money. Keynes's innovation is based on a classificatory inversion.

Previously, money-of-account was an accidental representation of money-as-a-thing. Contrarily, Keynes ([1930] 2011: 3–5) defines money-as-a-thing (money-proper) as an accidental form of money-of-account. The genus is money-of-account, not money-proper: "Money-Proper ... can only exist in relation to a Money-of-Account" (ibid.: 3). Generating new knowledge about, and giving a new definition of, money can indeed be mastered by such simple logical operations. Under the condition that money-of-account is the genus of money, debt as well as prices and credit turn out to be the same as money because all three are numeral expressions of purchasing power (ibid.). The claim or notation of an amount of purchasing power someone owes to someone else, or someone wants to acquire, is already a connector of exchange and therefore money. Keynes thereby shows how money can be an immaterial link between exchange partners.

The material part of that connector, money-proper, is intentionally vaguely defined. "Money itself," Keynes writes ([1930] 2011: 3), is a "delivery of which debt-contracts and price-contracts are discharged." A discharging delivery could be an amount of dollars, a code word, or a pizza, depending on the contract. The only requirement is that there is a third whatever-it-is as a connector of exchange. Referring to a contract involving the weight of either the king of England or King George V, Keynes gives a charming explanation of materiality as a vague, second-order phenomenon of money (ibid.: 4). A particular case of that discharging delivery is a legal tender monopolizing the forms of money-proper and thereby the forms of accepted cash.

One might ask whether it is fruitful to subdivide money any further than into money-of-account and money-proper. Keynes ([1930] 2011: 3–5) attempts further diaeresis by introducing the different institutions that deal with or issue money. A much better distinction, however, is made by François Simiand ([1934] 2006), whose concept is virtually unknown because of his complicated style, although his thought is clear and distinct.[5] What Simiand calls *représentation monétaire* is in fact Keynesian money-of-account. It is divided into 'form' (*forme monétaire* or *forme de monnaie*) and 'expression' (*expression monétaire*). The form leads to 'monetary means' (*moyens monétaires*) that are 'money-proper' (*monnaie propre*) and 'fiat money' (*monnaie fiduciaire*), while the 'expression' can be subdivided into the 'meter' (*étalon monétaire*) and the *unité monétaire*, which represents the currency (as abstract form) as well as the numeral denominations. This distinction of form and expression is implicitly used by Keynes and should be the first analytic tool when a connector of exchange is identified. Simiand's conceptual refinement helps to clarify this primary distinction and leads to a clear-cut determination of which kind of money is used. Two sets of questions have to be answered. Concerning the expression of money, what is the currency, what are the numeral dimensions, and what is the meter? Concerning the form of money, what are the means of connectors? Are they given as money-proper or fiat money, as real value or value token based on trust (credit)? A precise description of every dimension of money in a particular society would be the reward for diligently answering these questions.

This short discussion of Keynes's and Simiand's diaeresis enables me to upgrade my first attempts to define money and reintegrate materiality and quantity. Plato's connector of exchange appears to have two parts: an abstract numeral element describing debt or purchasing power and a corresponding material element. To avoid the mistake of interpreting giving and counter-giving only as buying and selling, I propose to replace the term 'purchasing power' with the term 'expected amount of return'.

The relation between form and expression, between quantitative money-of-account and materialist money-proper, can be further conceptualized by integrating Aristotle's notions of potentiality (*dynamis*) and actuality (*energeia, entelecheia*) (cf. Aristotle 2003: 1046b27–1052a11). Debt has the potential to activate the full amount of money-proper if it is paid back completely, while money-proper as money *in actu* cannot provide its owner with a definitive answer to whether its purchasing power is based on the mere payback potential of a credit or on a real asset. The sum of both forms determines the current amount of monetary value in circulation, but an incorrect proportion between them is likely to cause economic problems in exchange relations of over- and underestimation and in dishonest and honest commerce. Too much monetary potential sets more connectors between people than assets assuring value. However, such an unlimited money potential can just be cut off, for instance, by debt relief, before becoming money-proper. Thus, from such a perspective, financial markets are not dangerous per se as long as they are detached from the economic sector producing real value. Money saved is also somehow money potential, because the potential exchange connector does not connect any exchange and thereby remains inactive. An exaggerated amount of money-proper was already described as a credit crunch and a liquidity trap by Keynes himself ([1936] 2008: 68–79; [1930] 2011: 1:123–133, 171–185; 2:95–148). At least for modern economies, a certain amount of non-realized money potential should be available. Hyper-inflation suddenly appears as a dangerously vexed situation. During a period of inflation, there is both too much value (or money) potential and not enough money-proper. From the perspective of the above diaeresis, inflation is thus a situation with not enough cash. The good handling of money is, therefore, prudently managing the ratio between money potential and actual money to harmonize form and expression by balancing the materiality and quantity of money in order to keep exchanges connected.

## Conclusion

As discovered in our dialogue, money is neither an object with three or four functions, nor a mode of thought, as Spengler proposed. Money, as my discussion of Plato and Aristotle suggested, is a non-object based in human action, a connector of exchange and a means without an end. In such a teleological approach to money's nature, quantity and materiality are properties. Although not the defining essential properties, they are key features determining the quality of usage of money. Examining Keynes, I identified quantity, or money-of-account, as the immaterial form of that exchange connector performed as debt and credit that is revealed as the genus of money in its material form and not its opposite, dematerialized form. The material form of that connector is money-proper in the sense of cash. In order to determine the relationship between both, I introduced Aristotle's concepts of actuality and potentiality. From that perspective, Spengler's cultural typology also becomes clearer. Magian civilizations are constrained to a mental level that prohibits even the possibility of having the potential to activate money *in actu*. Apollinian civilizations insist on stable actuality, while modern money is a project of mobilizing money's full potential. The proposed typology thereby provides three possible modes of imbalanced action patterns toward money.

As I suggested above, with reference to the Hellenic discussion of the 'ethical', the main challenge is to find guiding principles and good practices to harmonize the potentiality and actuality of money. In that sense, money is a matter of ethics but not of morality. The projected goodness is a well-functioning connector of exchange according to a purpose such as getting rich or providing a just distribution within society. To master this challenge well, action-orientated pragmatic sciences are needed to teach cleverness and prudence. The monetary system can change only if humans, who are its foundation, change their behavior.

_____

**Emanuel Seitz** completed his PhD at the University of Amsterdam and lives in Frankfurt as an independent scholar. His research investigates the relevance of prudence and cunning for modern social and political theory. With Hans Peter Hahn and Mario Schmidt, he has edited Mauss's treatises on money, published as *Schriften zum Geld* (2015). Recently, he published his PhD as "List und Form: Über Klugheit" (2019).

## Notes

1. This translation is by Charles F. Atkinson (see Spengler 1926). The translations of Plato, Aristotle, and Marx are my own.
2. This is my own translation. Atkinson translated this statement as "Classical Wealth does not consist in having possessions, but in piling money." However, 'Guthaben' signifies 'credit balance' and not 'having possessions'.
3. For a recent critique of modern mathematical economics, see Sedláček (2012: 353–369).
4. For the essential similarity of gift and money, see Schmidt (2014: 243–255). For the ambiguity of objects, see Ross (2014).
5. For a recent discussion on Simiand, see Mauss (2015: 64–120, 223–225).

## References

Arendt, Hannah. (1958) 1998. *The Human Condition*. 2nd ed. Chicago: University of Chicago Press.

Arestis, Philip, and Malcolm Sawyer, eds. 2006. *A Handbook of Alternative Monetary Economics*. Cheltenham: Edward Elgar.

Aristotle. 2003. *Metaphysik*. Trans. Hans G. Zekl. Würzburg: Königshausen & Neumann.

Aristotle. 2006. *77 Tricks zur Steigerung der Staatseinnahmen. Oikonomika II*. Trans. Kai Brodersen. Stuttgart: Reclam.

Aristotle. 2007. *Nikomachische Ethik*. Trans. Olof Gigon. Düsseldorf: Artemis & Winkler.

Aristotle. 2012. *Politik*. Trans. Eckart Schütrumpf. Hamburg: Meiner.

Bohannan, Paul. 1955. "Some Principles of Exchange and Investment among the Tiv." *American Anthropologist* 57 (1): 60–70.

Brodbeck, Karl-Heinz. 2012. *Die Herrschaft des Geldes: Geschichte und Systematik*. Darmstadt: Wissenschaftliche Buchgesellschaft.

Crespo, Ricardo F. 2013. *Theoretical and Practical Reason in Economics: Capacities and Capabilities*. Dordrecht: Springer.

Crespo, Ricardo F. 2014. *A Re-Assessment of Aristotle's Economic Thought.* London: Routledge.

Dodd, Nigel. 2014. *The Social Life of Money.* Princeton, NJ: Princeton University Press.

Dostaler, Gilles. 2007. *Keynes and His Battles.* Trans. Niall B. Mann. Cheltenham: Edward Elgar.

Einzig, Paul. 1951. *Primitive Money: In Its Ethnological, Historical and Economic Aspects.* London: Eyre & Spottiswoode.

European Central Bank. 2015. "Monetary Developments in the Euro Area: January 2015." Press release, 26 February. https://www.ecb.europa.eu/press/pdf/md/md1501.pdf.

Gerloff, Wilhelm. 1952. *Geld und Gesellschaft: Versuch einer gesellschaftlichen Theorie des Geldes.* Frankfurt: Klostermann.

Graeber, David. 2011. *Debt: The First 5,000 Years.* Brooklyn, NY: Melville House.

Hart, Keith. 2012. "The Persuasive Power of Money." In *Economic Persuasions*, ed. Stephen Gudeman, 136–158. New York: Berghahn Books.

Heidegger, Martin. (1924) 2002. *Grundbegriffe der aristotelischen Philosophie.* Frankfurt: Klostermann.

Heinsohn, Gunnar, and Otto Steiger. 2002. *Eigentum, Zins und Geld: Ungelöste Rätsel der Wirtschaftswissenschaft.* Marburg: Metropolis.

Jevons, W. Stanley. 1896. *Money and the Mechanism of Exchange.* New York: Appleton.

Kant, Immanuel. (1800) 2004. *Lectures on Logic.* Trans. and ed. J. Michael Young. Cambridge: Cambridge University Press.

Keynes, John M. (1930) 2011. *A Treatise on Money.* Mansfield Centre: Martino Publishing.

Keynes, John M. (1936) 2008. *General Theory of Employment, Interest and Money.* New Delhi: Atlantic Publishers.

Laum, Bernhard. 1924. *Heiliges Geld: Eine historische Untersuchung über den sakralen Ursprung des Geldes.* Tübingen: Mohr.

MacIntyre, Alasdair. (1981) 2013. *After Virtue.* London: Bloomsbury.

Marx, Karl. (1867) 2007. *Das Kapital.* Berlin: Karl Dietz.

Mauss, Marcel. 2015. *Schriften zum Geld.* Ed. Hans Peter Hahn. Berlin. Suhrkamp.

Menger, Carl. (1909) 1970. "Geld." In *Gesammelte Werke*, ed. Friedrich Hayek, 1–117. Tübingen: Mohr.

Paul, Axel T. 2012. *Die Gesellschaft des Geldes: Entwurf einer monetären Theorie der Moderne.* Wiesbaden: Verlag für Sozialwissenschaften.

Plato. 2005. *Der Staat.* Trans. Friedrich Schleiermacher. Darmstadt: Wissenschaftliche Buchgesellschaft.

Polanyi, Karl. 1944. *The Great Transformation: The Political and Economic Origins of Our Time.* Boston: Beacon Press.

Redman, Deborah A. 2003. *The Rise of Political Economy as a Science: Methodology and the Classical Economists.* Cambridge, MA: MIT Press.

Ross, Sandy. 2014. "What Is Ambiguous about Ambiguous Goods?" *Journal of Consumer Behaviour* 13 (2): 140–147.

Sahlins, Marshall. 1972. *Stone Age Economics.* Chicago: Aldine-Atherton.

Schmidt, Mario. 2014. *Wampum und Biber: Fetischgeld im kolonialen Nordamerika: Eine mausssche Kritik des Gabeparadigmas.* Bielefeld: Transcript.

Sedláček, Tomáš. 2012. *Die Ökonomie von Gut und Böse.* Munich: Hanser. Originally published as *Ekonomie dobra a zla* in 2009 in Czech.

Simiand, François. (1934) 2006. "La monnaie, réalité sociale." In *Critique sociologique de l'économie*, ed. Jean-Christophe Marcel and Philippe Steiner, 213–259. Paris: Presses Universitaires de France.

Simmel, Georg. (1900) 2004. *The Philosophy of Money*. Trans. David Frisby. London: Routledge.

Simmel, Georg. (1900) 2009. *Philosophie des Geldes*. Cologne: Anaconda.

Sloterdijk, Peter. 2012. *Du mußt dein Leben ändern: Über Anthropotechnik*. Berlin: Suhrkamp.

Smith, Adam. (1776) 2007. *An Inquiry into the Nature and Causes of the Wealth of Nations*. Ed. by Sávio M. Soares. Amsterdam: MetaLibri.

Spengler, Oswald. (1923) 1963. *Der Untergang des Abendlandes: Umrisse einer Morphologie der Weltgeschicht*. Munich: Beck.

Spengler, Oswald. 1926. *The Decline of the West*. Trans. Charles F. Atkinson. New York: Knopf.

Wagner, Tim, and Christof Rapp. 2004. "Einleitung." In Aristotle, *Topik*, ed. Tim Wagner and Christof Rapp, 7–42. Stuttgart: Reclam.

Yuran, Noam. 2014. *What Money Wants: An Economy of Desire*. Stanford, CA: Stanford University Press.

# AFTERWORD

*Nigel Dodd*

The history of monetary thought is littered with binary distinctions—commodity versus credit, personal versus impersonal, state versus market—that, although often misleading and unhelpful, continue to shape debates about the nature of money. But perhaps none is as foundational and as far-reaching as the opposition between quantity and quality. In my own discipline of sociology, it is hard to avoid concluding that money's primary impact on social life is to quantify. Classical social thought was stuffed full of arguments about the shattering consequences for modern Western society, especially during the nineteenth century when what Simmel's great editor, David Frisby, once called the 'mature money economy' grew in intensity and spread into areas of social life that were—so the argument went—hitherto untouched by money. Given Georg Simmel's (2004) claim that money makes us treat every social encounter as a mathematical problem, while Weber (1991: 331) characterized it as "the most abstract and 'impersonal' element that exists in human life," it is hardly surprising to find this ongoing process of 'monetization' in society being treated largely as bad news, both then and since.

References for this section begin on page 134.

Today, books and articles that depict money as socially corrosive *because* it quantifies are still being written and continue to generate widespread populist appeal. Best sellers such as *How Much Is Enough?* by Robert and Edward Skidelsky (2012) and *What Money Can't Buy* by Michael Sandel (2013) frame our obsession with money as symptomatic of a pathological society. Even Pope Francis joined the chorus of complaint against the cultural damage that can be inflicted by money, lambasting neo-liberalism as the "dictatorship of the economy without purpose nor a truly human face" and arguing that "the ancient worship [of] the golden calf has found a new and ruthless image in fetishism of money" (Aguirre 2013). For anyone seeking a more nuanced, textured interpretation of money that takes full account of its qualitative characteristics, this is depressing stuff.

Either/or-ism of any kind is troubling, however, and we must be careful not to veer from what Zelizer (2011: 314) rightly decries as a tendency to exclude qualitative features of money completely from our analysis and to treat money as "nothing but culture, [or] nothing but politics." A similar point is made by Philippe Steiner (2009: 103)—against Zelizer, as it happens—when he applauds Karl Polanyi for equipping us with the critical weapons for appreciating the full impact of the quantitative side of money, especially in the context of neo-liberalism. One of the most intriguing aspects of money is that it is capable of expressing contrasting and even apparently contradictory aspects of social and economic life. These are not contradictions in our understanding of money that need to be resolved by smart theory. Rather, they are different sides of money that co-exist simultaneously, enabling us to enjoy a relationship with it that is as rich and rewarding as it is damaging and problematic. Hence, we need to think more dialectically about money. Money can be celebrated as something joyful and irrational, emotional and personal—not understood only as cold, hard, and impersonal. And it can, as Schmidt's chapter skillfully shows, be just as much a symbol of coercion as a vehicle of empowerment.

Likewise, it does not suffice to continue treating the quantitative and qualitative aspects of money as if they exist in a relationship of blissful mutual exclusivity. As I argue in *The Social Life of Money* (Dodd 2014: 294–305), one major flaw in debates of this kind is the tendency to lock the quantitative features of money inside a black box, as if all dollars are equal (to paraphrase Zelizer) simply because spending them involves counting. Or to express this point from the other direction, it is as if all calculation is the same; *ergo*, all dollars will be the same. The classical literature was full of brilliant insights into how money can flatten and deaden our world by rendering it measurable, transforming quality into quantity. Marx called money the "radical leveler" that "extinguishes all distinctions" (1982: 229) and "makes impossibilities fraternize" (2000: 118). Nietzsche (1996: 51) equated the setting of prices with "thinking as such," while Simmel (2004: 444) said that the money economy "enforces the necessity of continuous mathematical operations in our daily transactions." The problem with these insights, however, is that they are so one-sided, as if this were all that money ever does and will continue to do in the same way.

The lasting significance of the work of anthropologists such as Jane Guyer—and, I believe, the great achievement of the chapters in this edited volume—is to get inside that black box in order to show that calculation must be studied from the inside and understood, for example, as a cultural index that is every bit as rich and textured as phenomena such as earmarking. Drawing from ethnographic research that she conducted in Cameroon and Nigeria, Guyer (2004) skillfully explores a complex and dynamic intermixing of quantity with quality that is unsystematic and 'wild'. As she makes clear, it is not a question of quantity versus quality. Rather, these are closely intertwined and dynamically interdependent standards of value. Perhaps such accounts of money are less immediately appealing beyond academia because they resist easy summary; indeed, they fail—rightly, in my view—to reach any hard and fast conclusions about the nature of money in general. The relationship between the quantitative and qualitative sides of money is not something that can be theorized; it must be painstakingly researched and carefully described.

As Ross, Schmidt, and Koskinen point out in the introduction, money does not simply measure quantities: it represents and symbolizes them in multiple, complex, and fascinating ways. Moreover, the chapters gathered here make an important move that is found too seldom in the burgeoning literature on the social, cultural, and political aspects of money. Instead of advancing qualitatively rich accounts of money that stand against the emerging 'quantitative turn' in the social sciences—characterized by an emphasis on Big Data and focusing on topics such as algorithmic trading—these chapters seek to contribute to this phenomenon by enriching it. In the analysis of money, one important aspect of such enrichment must be to move away from an almost obsessive focus on *haute* finance that tends to feature in the social studies of finance literature—as excellent as much of this work undoubtedly is—to explore, as the editors put it in the introduction, "how the enumeration of money's purchasing power is negotiated by ordinary people in everyday life." This is an aspect of money that tends to be underplayed, so the detailed treatment of it in this book is very welcome.

In drawing our attention to 'everyday' aspects of money, these chapters are consistent with a developing substantive trend within the monetary literature, namely, to focus on the emergence of monetary forms and practices that depart from the standard, homogenized monetary landscape that characterized much of the modern era in the West. What we have been witnessing since the early 1970s is the slow (but, I believe, inevitable) decline of the hegemony of national monies. I do not think that it is an exaggeration to see this is a significant moment of realignment in the world's monetary landscape. The era in which money was defined exclusively by the state has come to an end. Alternative and complementary currencies are growing at an astonishing rate today, and we need a greater range of conceptual tools in order to understand them, not least because they all have a different relationship with the representation and calculation of value. While some of these new monetary forms tend merely to imitate existing national currencies by utilizing their monies of account and remaining convertible into those currencies at a ratio of one to one, many of them do not; rather, they draw their scales of value from other phenomena such as time, labor, or reputation.

This increasing variation in the quantitative features of the monies we encounter on an everyday basis poses some interesting problems because it is inevitable that efforts will be made to render them commensurable. This need not necessarily mean that more standardization is inevitable. This is not a one-way process in either direction—toward variation on one side or standardization on the other. Instead, as I am suggesting, we need to think more dialectically about money. We therefore have much to learn from these chapters, which explore a rich repertoire of monetary scales. Let me be clear that I am not claiming that this kind of variance is especially new. What we are witnessing today, with the development of alternative and complementary monetary forms, is a return to a past in which money was much more plural than it has been throughout the modern era. Outside the global North, juggling with multiple scales of monetary value is a routine feature of everyday economic life, as the work of Guyer and others has shown.

Perhaps this explains the tendency for Western scholars to 'other' monetary multiplicity, as if it were a characteristic mainly of 'pre-modern' societies, where money is held to conform more closely to Polanyi's description of limited-purpose money. As the editors of this collection suggest, Polanyi's distinction seems to perpetuate the notion that only pre-modern or non-Western (limited-purpose) monies possess sufficient cultural richness to constitute objects of anthropological research in their own right, whereas later (general-purpose) monies correspond to the culturally neutral, colorless media of exchange that is proposed by descriptions of it as a homogeneous tool of calculation. Although Polanyi's main criticism of orthodox treatments of money is that they are too narrow, he based this critique on evidence from non-market societies. So it is by exploring "new dimensions of money's quantities" (introduction, this volume) that these chapters make their own specific and valuable contribution to the understanding of contemporary monies. If what anthropologists call the 'substantivist' view of money applies anywhere, it surely applies everywhere. Peter Oakley (this volume) expresses the point so well: "Money as a total abstraction cannot actually be studied at all."

So how does the qualitative study of money's quantitative properties actually work, and what does it tell us? As these chapters variously show, social and cultural practices shape money—from the inside, as it were—as a tool of calculation. Among other things, money helps people to codify and to rank, to put things (and each other) into hierarchies, and to sustain and reproduce social differences. This is a morally rich, as well as problematic, practice, as the chapter by Holbraad clearly demonstrates. That there is nothing new in this can be seen even from the most cursory glance at the history of money, where for example, practices associated with wergild, or 'man price' (see Echterhölter, this volume) feature prominently. Found at various points in monetary history, these practices involved the quantification of social differences by levying fines for personal injuries: wergild was not simply a means of measuring harm done, but of codifying social order (see Hudson 2004). The chapters in this volume resonate with this example, while at the same time showing that such practices are not just old, but very contemporary indeed. This point is brilliantly conveyed in the chapters by Anna Echterhölter, Sandy Ross, and Martin Fotta.

A collection that is as richly descriptive as this one makes theoretical generalizations about the nature of money as a tool of calculation and measurement difficult to sustain. Empirically, they make it necessary to treat money as an open site, where the significance and impact of its quantitative functions are best regarded as a research question, not as matters for theoretical presumption. Having said this, what the chapters gathered here do so well is to maintain important threads in the theoretical literature about money, perhaps none more so than the chapter by Emanuel Seitz. In other words, these chapters are not merely descriptive, but open up some significant and potentially far-reaching analytical questions about what money does when we use it to quantify things. Above all, they show that money's calculative features are an integral, variable, and socially rich aspect of its qualities as a medium.

**Nigel Dodd** is a Professor in the Sociology Department at the London School of Economics and Political Science (LSE). He obtained his PhD from the University of Cambridge in 1991 and lectured at the University of Liverpool before joining the LSE in 1995. His research focuses on the sociology of money, economic sociology, and classical and contemporary social thought. His publications include *The Sociology of Money* (1994), *Social Theory and Modernity* (1999), and, most recently, *The Social Life of Money* (2014).

## References

Aguirre, Estefania. 2013. "'Money Has to Serve, Not Rule!' Pope Tells New Ambassadors." *Catholic News Agency*, 16 May. https://www.catholicnewsagency.com/news/money-has-to-serve-not-rule-pope-tells-new-ambassadors.

Dodd, Nigel. 2014. *The Social Life of Money*. Princeton, NJ: Princeton University Press.

Guyer, Jane I. 2004. *Marginal Gains: Monetary Transactions in Atlantic Africa*. Chicago: University of Chicago Press.

Hudson, Michael. 2004. "The Archaeology of Money: Debt Versus Barter Theories of Money's Origins." In *Credit and State Theories of Money: The Contributions of A. Mitchell Innes*, ed. L. Randall Wray, 99–127. Cheltenham: Edward Elgar.

Marx, Karl. 1982. *Capital*. Vol. 1: *A Critique of Political Economy*. Trans. Ben Fowkes. London: Penguin.

Marx, Karl. 2000. "Economic and Philosophical Manuscripts." In *Marx: Selected Writings*, ed. David McLellan, 83–120. Oxford: Oxford University Press.

Nietzsche, Friedrich. 1996. *On the Genealogy of Morals*. Trans. Douglas Smith. Oxford: Oxford University Press.

Sandel, Michael J. 2013. *What Money Can't Buy: The Moral Limits of Markets*. London: Penguin.

Simmel, Georg. 2004. *The Philosophy of Money: Third Enlarged Edition*. Ed. David Frisby; trans. Tom Bottomore and David Frisby. London: Routledge.

Skidelsky, Robert, and Edward Skidelsky. 2012. *How Much Is Enough? Money and the Good Life*. New York: Other Press.

Steiner, Philippe. 2009. "Who Is Right about the Modern Economy: Polanyi, Zelizer, or Both?" *Theory and Society* 38 (1): 97–110.

Weber, Max. 1991. *From Max Weber*. Ed. Bryan S. Turner. London: Routledge.

Zelizer, Viviana A. 2011. *Economic Lives: How Culture Shapes the Economy*. Princeton, NJ: Princeton University Press.

# INDEX

abstraction
    money's potential of, 1, 2, 67, 94, 103,
        109
    numbers and, 30, 60, 100, 125
    total, 18, 133
acquire or demonstrate strength (força),
    9, 105
actions, symbolic, 35–36
affordances, 78
ambiguity
    of measurement, 32, 34, 40
    of money chain, 2, 23, 28
    of relation to money, 67
Apollinian economics, 117, 118
arbitrage, 103
Aristotle, 119, 125, 126
    on monetary theory, 120, 121, 122,
        123
arithmetic divisibility, 4–5, 12
    of money, 50–51, 54, 71
    recursive divisibility conflicted with,
        3–4, 53–54
auction, 11, 25, 75–76

bank notes, 1, 18, 50–60
barbarian laws (leges barbarorum), 39, 41
barter, 5, 120
basic needs, 88, 90, 119
binary license, 81–82, 93–94
blood money, 32, 40, 43
body weight, in gold, 41, 43
Bohannan, Laura and Paul, 60, 61
boundaries, quantity-quality, 11, 12, 51,
    62, 131

Brazil
    Calons in, 98, 99, 100, 102–108, 110,
        112n4, 112n6, 112n8
    Ciganos in, 99. 103, 110–111
    Gypsy money in, 3, 8–9
    Jurons in, 98, 99, 104, 107
bribes, 22, 73–74

calculation, 58–60, 89, 93, 109, 117, 132
    devices of, 3, 57
    fuzzy, 51, 59
    money as a tool of, 133–134
    suspension of, 100
Calon (Brazilian Gypsies), 98, 112n4,
        112n6, 112n8
    debts of, 106
    domestic economies of, 104
    loans of, 107, 108
    on monetary sums, 99, 100, 102, 105,
        110
    as moneylenders, 12, 103
capital, 72–75
capitalist economy, 5, 62, 88
categories of thought, 116–117, 118, 119
chance, 36–37, 43, 44
chopin, la. See dollar shops
Ciganos (Brazilian Gypsies), 99, 103,
        110–111
    See also Calon (Brazilian Gypsies)
codes, of rural law, 33, 34, 43
coinage, precious metal, 18–19
combinatory numerical practices, 73
Comedy of Errors, The (Shakespeare),
    22–23

future, 5–6, 72–73, 78, 118
　making of, 104, 105
　orientation, 54, 101

Gabori Roma (Romanian Gypsies), 101,
　102
gambling, 101, 105
*ganhador* (one who gains), 98
Gaźos (non-Gypsies, Hungary), 101
*General Theory of Employment, Interest
　and Money* (Keynes), 123
gift
　economy, 123
　exchanges, 6
giving and counter-giving (*metadidomi*),
　119–120
gold, 18
　body weight in, 41, 43
　jewelry, 2, 11
　price fluctuation of, 23–24
　standard, 103
　weight used for jewelry, 27
gold jewelry, 2, 11
　hallmark system of, 26
　as money, 27
　as scrap, 24–25
　specie compared to, 20
Graeber, David, 40–41, 115
Grierson, Philip, 39–40
Grimm, Jacob, 36
　on controllable measurement, 37
　on injury measurement, 41, 43
　on procedural measurements, 31–32,
　　33–34, 38, 43–44
　on theory of measurements, 35
　on wergild system, 41, 42, 43
Guyer, Jane, 32–33, 60, 132
Gypsies. *See* Calon (Brazilian Gypsies);
　Ciganos (Brazilian Gypsies);
　Gabori Roma (Romanian Gypsies);
　Vlach Rom (Hungarian Gypsies)

*habaneros* (people of Havana), 86, 87, 91
hallmark system, of gold jewelry, 26
hard currency, 84
heap, paradox of, 9, 10
heuristics, of affluent migrants, 49–50,
　52, 53, 58–59, 61
high finance, 2
hoards, 108, 110, 118
　national reserve as, 103–104

*homo oeconomicus*, 2
household preservation, 68, 102
Hungary
　non-Gypsies (Gaźos non-Gypsies) in,
　　101
　Romani and Vlach Rom Gypsies in,
　　99, 101, 102
hysteresis, 9–10, 11, 105–106

infinity, 6–8, 67–69, 70–71, 77–78
inflation, 126
injuries
　Grimm on, 41, 43
　measuring, 38–39
interest rates, 75, 107, 117
invisible hand, 19

jewelry, 20–21, 23
　musters of, 24–25
　*See also* gold jewelry
jewelry collections
　currency compared with, 27–28
　as meta-objects, 25, 26
Jurons (Brazilian non-Gypsies), 98, 99,
　104, 105–111
justice, and monetary theory, 119, 120,
　121

Kenyatta, Uhuru, 68
Keynes, John M., 114, 116, 123–125, 126

law
　Germanic, 32, 39, 45n3
　Luo, 74
*leges barbarorum. See* barbarian laws
Lévi-Strauss, Claude, 3
liquidity, 23, 26, 107, 126
loans, of Calon, 107, 108
*lucha. See* struggle
Luo culture, 74, 76, 77

Malaby, Thomas M., 58
management, of divisible cash, 52–53
man price. *See* wergild
marginality, 12, 101
market
　economy, 123
　exchange, 40
　financial, 8, 126
　free, 19
Marx, Karl, 117, 131